RAVEN SMITH'S
TRIVIAL PURSUITS

RAVEN SMITH'S TRIVIAL PURSUITS

RAVEN SMITH

4th ESTATE • *London*

4th Estate
An imprint of HarperCollins*Publishers*
1 London Bridge Street
London SE1 9GF

www.4thEstate.co.uk

First published in Great Britain in 2020 by 4th Estate

1

Set in Adobe Garamond Pro
Printed and bound in Great Britain by
CPI Group (UK) Ltd, Croydon

Rather than a dedication, it's more fitting
to start with two apologies.

Firstly, to my mum on account of how
much I talk about my cock.

And secondly, to my husband on account
of how much I talk about his.

Contents

A Trivial Pursuit

Forrest Gump was wrong: life is nothing like a box of chocolates, it's more like drunk-biting into a kebab on the night bus. You're trying to Jay Rayner the different flavour profiles but they're mashed between pitta and the top deck's swirling while you grip your door key between your knuckles, refusing to black out before your stop. Is that a curl of doner meat or a piece of napkin you've hungry-caterpillared? Like a kebab, our lives have countless ingredients; the dominant flavours and hidden additives are interlocking, co-dependant parts, like a thirtieth-birthday Omega. Disparate life-stuff vies for our attention like listening to three podcasts and a voicenote as the sound of dial-up internet reverberates backwards on a Sonos. There's a consensus that life and death and kids really do matter. But we've also Googled *beach sandals* and *healing crystals* and *carbs in a mango*. These things matter too, but in a different way to voter fraud or organised religion or melting ice caps. Those little pots of chunked parmesan at Whole Foods feel a touch frivolous when compared to famine. The Pizza

Express dough balls don't cancel out genocide. Having to queue for too long at a bar boils my piss, but gin and tonic is a welcome distraction from our current political hell. These small things are inconsequential, but we chase them. Our trivial pursuits.

It's helpful to think of life as a Monet – a canvas layered with splodgy strokes. A masterpiece *and* a big old mess. There's just a lot of stuff to consider: your height, your weight, your jeans, your genes. Your education, your privilege, your subscription to the *New Yorker*. Can you still eat avocados? Can you still eat salmon? Can you still drink tap water? Or Aperol? Or probiotic yoghurt? Ottolenghi, easyJet, immigration. Joni Mitchell, the McCanns, Kim Kardashian. #MeToo and the 5:2. Microbeads in the sea. A starving polar bear on a splinter of iceberg. Can you be a good person if you don't devote your life to Greenpeace? Can you be a good person without an asylum seeker in your spare bedroom? Can you be a good person and still judge the dresses at the Met Gala? Is pink back? Is pink woke? Is pink naff because it got woke and then we ruined it? How do you even pronounce Moët? Are we running out of time? Are we running out of resources? Are we running out of waitresses because of Brexit? Life's torrential downpour of dust-bunnies under your bed piles up on the surfaces like Miss Havisham's attic.

And are you engaging with it all? Or just scrolling down the feed liking pics? Are you actually getting happier? Or just less anxious? Are you making a good indelible mark on this planet, or leaving a cavernous carbon footprint? Are you the change you want to see in the world, or do you just tweet about it? Are you a muggle, commuting through life with your eyes down on today's paper? Are you a messiah preaching the gospel, or an obedient disciple? And when you finally get to the pearly gates of heaven, will that one viral tweet count for or against your entry?

Modern life is rubble. Shingle from the bottom of the ocean brought in by the tide. We comb the beach ascribing value to each discovery. Whether that's eating McDonald's or living vegan, Donna Tartt or emojis, David Hockney or Zoella, being healthy or being thin. These are the trivialities we chase, our aspirations outside of having kids and not dying. We pursue these trifles that are both soufflé-light *and* anvil-heavy. At times they're as mundane as a Uniqlo sock, at others they're as dizzying as a diamond earring. We're riddled with choices like a gangrenous leg, but we don't have to be binary between the profound *or* the irrelevant. They coexist. These things have a meaning but they are also meaningless, overshadowed by genuine disasters.

Each decision we make is a self-portrait, but like Elizabethans we commission painters who make us look better. We don't choose stuff for who we are, but more for who we want to be, perusing a life we see as successful.

In most cases trivial pursuits aren't a conscious act by the participant. They're a complex, invisible system of influence, like the mafia. And quiet prompts steer us from the periphery of our vision. Like most fairytales, this book is based on a simple conceit: everything in your life is trivial, but also has enough meaning to pursue. The small stuff is straw, but like Rumpelstiltskin the straw is also the gold. Take shoes, for example. If you see a pair of shoes online you may ask yourself, 'Do I want these shoes?' It's innocuous enough. But within that question you're like Cinderella, a woman who transformed her whole life with the perfect shoe and partied hard and fell in love. But the question has doubt too. You're the undeserving ugly sister coveting the shoe. Do you deserve the shoe, or the prince? Should you buy the shoe for some future engagement at which you'll feel worthy of the shoe? Will wearing the shoe convince you and the people around you that you're worthy of the shoe? And in this whole shoe-mess you're also Prince Charming. You're searching for the woman who wears this shoe.

Does that make sense? It sounds ridiculous because it is. And we're all doing it all the time, with multiple decisions we make about our time and our houses and our baby names and our dick pics. A million micro-factors encouraging us to *do* more and *be* more. We're all striving for something, whether it's a great meal, or the right hand-soap, or a cute kid with tiny Birkenstocks (always the right shoe). Everything is a major or minor decision, made en route to this bigger portrait we're painting of who we *really* are.

I heard on *Woman's Hour* that life is a big U shape: happy childhood at the start, and happy old age, the middle a big sag where you mainly just work and eat, and worry about money and worry about food. This book, I think, is the bottom of the U, all the human existing that congregates in the reservoir tip before we hit the blissful slalom of old age. Sometimes the U is filling with water and we're drowning rats clawing up the sides, other times it's a hammock and we're lazing on a sunny afternoon.

I lie awake thinking about a bag of crisps I opened upside down last year, but alongside that there are more frets. Is empathy in retrograde? Do we care more about ourselves than other people? Am I middle-class-signalling by shopping at Waitrose? What if I only buy own-brand goods there? Is that actually worse? How is time passing so quickly? How is time passing so slowly? Why am I tired all the time? On my deathbed will I wish I'd slept more? After I die will they make a twelve-part Netflix original about me? Who will play me if Meryl is busy? Who will play me if Meryl is dead? What is my legacy? What is my lunch? Do I fail every time I eat carbs? Or do I beat the system? Could I perform the Heimlich manoeuvre in an emergency despite never having been taught it? Why am I sweating when I'm sitting still? Why am I back scrolling Instagram? Why do I pretend to hate the internet, and that an analogue life is a more pious path? Is sass a superpower or an Achilles heel? Is charm real? Is charisma real? Are these traits you're born with? Or do you cultivate them like a garden? Deep down in my soul, in the bit you can't see in selfies, am I the cat bin lady, angrily and chaotically acting out at the world? Or am I the cat in the bin, manhandled without my consent? Am I the bin itself, passively filled by nearby drama? I've lost hours searching for rugby-striped bedding, which is as much to do with my religious love of John Lewis as it is about the reminiscence of being a closet gay in a rugby scrum at school. What does getting the right bedding really mean on my personal success scale? Do I even notice most of my achievements? Or are they all passing clouds? When I die, will some zany acquaintance insist everyone wears colourful clothes to my funeral? That would be really bad.

I'm not concerned with how we got here, I'm interested in the status quo. I'm not going to trace back to our penny-farthinged pre-internet culture, nor am I going to Charlie Brooker your future. This book will not tell you how to feel. When to cry. When to laugh. When to panic. You don't get a gold star for reading two lines without checking you phone in between. This book is a buffet, but unlike the lukewarm salmonella-y kind, there are plenty of piping-hot takes. I will keep serving dishes as you Bruce Bogtrotter them. I have a lot of questions. Is being tall its own social currency? Am I the contents of my fridge? Does plastic recycling matter if we all still eat fish? Does yoga matter if you're not filthy rich? Am I the Nelson Mandela of Grindr because I managed to escape it? Is this the long walk to monogamy? Will I ever be as hot as I was on my wedding day? Will I ever be as hungry? Is a bagel four slices of bread? Are vitamin supplements secret carbs? Are three cigarettes a meal? Fucking hell, Raven, a meal is a meal.

Raven Smith's Trivial Pursuits answers some of these questions, and reflects on the importance of the least important things. A CSI dark light that shows you the ominous stains of our frivolous attempts to accomplish or attain. Tie a napkin round your neck, *chérie*, and I'll provide the rest.

The Fear

As someone who's never done a live sex show, I can say with confidence that nothing gives you performance anxiety like sitting down to write a book. When starting this book I was riddled with apprehension, the kind that paralyses you and freezes you mid-scene like porn on a bad internet connection. I've had intense jobs before, all the palaver of contract negotiation and emails flying back and forth like a gravel pit. A meaningful work project takes infinite energy and infinite patience, but the end result is worth every brave conversation, every 7 a.m. conference call, every stand-up argument across the open-plan office. The time I threw a shoe. The time I 'humiliated' the cleaner. That little slap for the intern. A meaningful project is worth settling out of court. But every work meltdown before today was a merry Morris dance, all belled shoes and ribboned sticks, compared to the actuality of having to write this book. I will never say I'm overwhelmed again.

Like a self-professed *summer person*, schvitzing in the corner with a wet top lip as the humidity peaks, I declared myself a *book person*, thinking it was a personality I could slather on like sun cream. But when summer hit I just felt sweaty and stressed like wilted salad leaves left out of the fridge. Writing a book about modern life while living a modern life is basically declaring yourself the puppet who wants to be the puppeteer. Not just a Pinocchio participant in culture, but an observer of all the strings that hold it up – Geppetto overseeing the whole dance with strategic tugs to the beat. My bravado simmered down and the doubt crept in the way a summer anthem infects your brain. Could I even write? What defines an essay? Could I pose a juicy question? Then illuminate an answer? Could I show the judges versatility too? Beyond that, could I do daring literary gymnastics like Shakespeare on a pill? If all the world's a stage, was I ready to tap dance? Not sonnets. I didn't want to write sonnets because they're a bit old-fashioned. But could I write a book for normal people who just want a little jazz?

Writers have always held a particular allure, because they aren't like regular people. Writers don't just observe the world like it's streaming on Netflix: they masticate the world, they ingest it, and it marinates, eventually thrown up as a warm flume of hot takes. Out of them trails a festoon of delicate-but-robust prose, like a string of knotted hankies from Fagin's pocket. It felt bold to call myself a writer. More of a hypothesis than a fact. A thrill cut through with potential humiliation, like a beery teenage kiss. I feel like an interloper, climbing aboard the literary boat like the

Somali pirates on Tom Hanks's container ship. I'm the writer now.

But I've scrambled my brain. Social media and the news cycle and infinite scrolling have whittled my attention span down to a nub. So while I'm triple-screening I'm also plotting, or coveting, or consuming. Every waking second brings an avalanche of ideas to sift through like the currants in a Christmas pudding while you search for the coin. Ideas dangle before my eyes like Boris Johnson on that zipline. Worries and desires and regrets stack up in my head. The sheer panic that I didn't fully cash in when I was a twink. The sheer panic that the Cosmopolitan cocktail won't make a comeback like the dinosaurs in *Jurassic Park*. The sheer panic that my dad was so laid-back as a parent I just absorbed complacency like a human kitchen towel. Is shopping a religious experience? Or are gyms the new churches? Why isn't there a Mumsnet for gays? Or a Grindr for meeting the best people at a party without having to wade through the bores?

Thoughts come as easily as teenage boys but bounce off just as quickly, refusing to stick around for a second date. I wanted to step back from the trillion passing thoughts and conduct them, or at least organise them into workable groups. To somehow jettison out of my head and orbit the mess, an astronaut weightlessly jotting down his observations. I began this book on a dictation app, endlessly pacing my kitchen ad-libbing into my phone like the Lenny Henry of Camberwell but without the Red Nose Day suit or the

Premier Inn deal. The notes caught thoughts like the trowel that came with our litter tray so you can sieve out the cat shit. I covertly spoke to the app everywhere I went, like a portable confessional booth. Cut to me in the street counter-arguing a podcast on my way to yoga. See me gurn-whispering into my phone in the corner of a club. I would wake just before dawn, with bin-breath, and express groggy observations right from the heart of my subconscious.

Countless things materialise when you're talking to yourself. One is that I say *essentially* a lot. And *basically*. And talk almost exclusively in metaphors. But a phrase jumped out of my notes: *Everything is a distraction from death*. I can be quite melodramatic – perhaps there's a teenage goth hiding inside me, all black boots and cobweb make-up. I still embrace this death sentiment, because everything *is* a distraction from death. We can either focus on the inevitable conclusion, or distract ourselves, gawping at the football streaker before the match ends. We find a way to fill that finite space between cradle and grave.

Before I typed a word I procrastinated. Procrastination is my toxic boyfriend, a confirmed bachelor keeping me from committing words to the page. The first bout of research had nothing to do with books. I was more concerned with how writers dress. I searched pictures of them at their desks and bought caricature garments. Sartorially, Truman Capote in Venice won out, all laid-back white shirts and wrinkled cords. Capote once said 'Venice is like eating an entire box of chocolate liqueurs in one go,' and I've always felt like that about my own personality: appetising and moreish at first, giving way to an overwhelming sickliness.

Wrinkled cords helped set the mood like a dimmer switch at a swingers' night, but I still couldn't sit down and type. Procrastination kept me scrolling pictures of Tripp Fontaine for hours. It helped me pick little fights with my husband by WhatsApping him pictures of his mess around the house. Procrastination was *sous chef* to the extravagant sandwiches I made for lunch that took forty-five minutes minimum to assemble. I produced pint after tart pint of 'Raven's Lemon Curd' which I gifted to friends. I talked about writing a lot, saying 'It's just a numbers game,' not knowing that that was a naïve lie. I quipped that I was an essayist, because even the word 'writer' became more and more loaded, a gun in my pocket about to shoot me in the foot. I decided that if I pretended to be confident I would become confident, like a birthday wish when you blow out the candles. In my most baller moments I convinced myself that I was the undiscovered voice of my generation, a phrase that leaves a metallic taste in your mouth like you've licked a fistful of coppers. I swallowed that acid idea down and let it settle in my stomach like Vesuvius ash. I watched my husband's poker face as I told him I was the voice of my generation, looking for a fault, for a wince, some sign we were colluding in the narcissism. He never faltered, because he knowns when to pick his battles and he doesn't want an arrow in the eye. Husbands can be very good at building momentum but they can also slam the brakes. This time he left me running like a car engine while he nipped in for a grab bag of Quavers to keep my blood sugar up. I sat in the passenger seat as the vehicle filled with toxic voice-of-a-generation-monoxide, breathing on the windshield and writing *voiceofageneration* in the mist. I said to my husband, 'I have to believe I'm the voice of my generation to write this book, it doesn't matter if it's true.' It felt empowering *and* deluded to say it, and thrilling to force him into secrecy. It was a pact that brought us closer, but I still didn't write a word. Instead I wrote 'voice of a generation?' in an email and saved it to drafts.

Shifting from audio note-taking to actual book-writing was like the early days of a love affair: anxious, confusing, obsessive, joyful, exhausting, exhilarating. I felt like I was sixteen again: self-conscious, besotted and confused, trying to convince myself not to obsess. Each day I sat down to edit my muddled thoughts, rather than facing the expectant blinking cursor of an empty Word doc. The anxiety of a blank page was forgotten, and I couldn't shut up about it. I could hear people getting bored with my book-fixation, but I couldn't stop. The process was electric and fluid, a hazardous and insoluble mix. Lively and dampening. I would find myself so sodden with anxiety I wanted to climb into a bag of rice. Forever. Unlike a love affair, there is no reciprocity. You pile more of yourself into the book and nothing comes back out. You are doing stand-up into the abyss. Transmitting but not receiving. One hand clapping in an echo chamber of your own notes.

The first sentence was the hardest, like pissing out a Sylvanian Families badger. I wanted to write something both humble and heroic to send out into the universe on a golden record. Something to misquote in the history books. Whatever I wrote would be a deliberate stain, an unsightly skidmark on new underwear, asylum seekers in Chipping Norton, pineapple on a pizza. Each sentence had to be written in red Sharpie that won't Cif off the fridge. Everything felt finite and irreversible. I was Nicole Kidman with a prosthetic nose (to make her look more Virginia Wolverine) lining her pockets with rocks and silently entering the water. Dragged to the bottom by the weight of the project. I cracked my knuckles, ready to expel magnificent observations and sparkling wit. Prose was constipated. I felt a hydraulic pressure to reveal something mundane that coincidentally-on-purpose tapped into a relatable zeitgeist below the surface of culture. A personal anecdote that would ripple out and touch countless lives. 'Let them eat cake' for the podcast generation, penned by Carrie Antoinette. The full-frontal exposure of my thoughts was daunting, like trying to open a tin of beans with a sharpened stick. It went beyond stagefright. The fear was a fatberg meandering the tunnels of my veins. I was the ninety-nine people in the room who didn't believe in me. All I had was wrinkled cords.

But then I wrote a sentence. An OK sentence. An everyday, palatable sentence. It wasn't *Let them eat Huel*, but it was good enough. And then I wrote another. I could nurture the seeds from the dictation app into seedlings, like a black Monty Don. I had paragraphs. And they were my bricks. I had blueprints and foundations, but I couldn't think ahead to the house I was building, because that was something for other people to peer into and walk around and judge. I was not ready for colour schemes or wallpaper or Kirsty Allsopp. But brick by brick I cornered off a little part of the world of my own. The wind changed direction and the skeleton of a building stayed standing. No huff and no puff. No subsidence. I have a tendency for complacency so I didn't look back, I kept my spirit level and I just kept writing.

Daytimes dragged, but similes Jackson Pollocked out of me late at night over Deliverooed Ben & Jerry's. Writing is like sex or exercise: you can overthink it, and spend too long getting down to it, but you hit a critical frenzied point and it feels amazing afterwards. Euphoric, near-orgasmic bouts of writing usually surface at 10 p.m., when I'd rather be having actual sex, when the black coffee is tepid and the ice cream is drinkable.

I found myself nit-combing my personal history, larvae and debris repurposed for chapters. Sometimes the writing is so hard I'm chiselling my own gravestone with my bare fingers. At other times an idea pours out like hot lava escaping a volcano and wiping out entire cities in its molten path. The book cannot be stopped. As easy as vomiting after you've eaten candyfloss and ridden the Wurlitzer: it's a simple equation of being overfull, and then shaken like a martini. The words projectile. Other times it's like puking on an empty stomach. All that straining and retching for half a mouthful of spit. I forced up metaphors for weeks, a form of verbal bulimia. Dehydrated and ruined, I considered calling NHS Direct. Thought-provoking copy can be extracted by careful caesarean, but you're not just the patient. I'm one of those Victorian surgeons you read about who operated on himself while trying to keep all the other organs ticking.

I'm gagging for a vacation from myself. A vacation from thinking. And from thinking about thinking. And thinking about the quality of my thoughts. And from worrying that I'm not thinking enough at all. Six weeks in the Bahamas in a medically-induced coma would suit, although I'm sure I'd find a way to dictate a few lines. Freddie Mercury said the show must go on, but how can anyone ever have gone through this process and not fallen to pieces? How can writers roam the earth without sinking into the quicksand of their own doubt? The fear gets louder: *You are not cut out for this. You're indulging yourself. You're only here as part of some diversity quota. You are undeserving.*

The sweetest escape is booze. I long to get annihilated by drink. Kamikaze drunk. George-Best-roaring-with-laughter drunk. *Scarface* high, but drunk. Hold-my-hair-back-and-paint-the-pavement-with-warm-tequila drunk. Lean-in-and-kiss-my-mate drunk. Lean-in-and-slap-my-mate drunk. That feeling of only being drunk, nothing in your head except *Don't fall over, don't throw up. Weekend at Bernie's*-walk-home-because-no-Uber-will-take-me drunk.

How do you solve a problem like tequila? I want to forget the seams of the chapters, the lyrics of the lines, the shape of the prose. Drink until I'm out of credit and can't send and receive text. I want to lose my voice and store it in a shell on the sea witch's neck. I want to wake up on the beach and comb my hair with a fork.

I don't get drunk. I don't wake up in A&E with charcoal round my lips. Like any good pessimist, I sit very still and worst-case-scenario plan. The dystopian Mystic Meg of my own life.

I can see a future where people tweet me about the book with concise little takedowns like *What the shit?* and *Who commissioned this garbage?* It's manageable at first, because I'm a big boy, and if I can handle bastard sewer rats wandering round my kitchen I can handle a few tweets. Initially I'm low-key proud, because trolls are a byproduct of fame, and this is clearly my fifteen minutes. A few aggy DMs cut to the bone because underneath the Acne bomber I'm a soft-shell crab, so despite sensible advice from people I love and trust, and specific case studies to the contrary, I engage with these haters. I fire out pithy tweets that immediately get torn to shreds by the rabble like chicken in a burrito. I feed these trolls giant nuggets of retort and morsels of badly-worded self-defence. The trolling is relentless in a way that can't be wittily anecdoted at dinner parties. People look at me with the head tilt you do when you know someone's recovering from the flu. Some troll sets up a bot that tweets each line from the book with 'Cancel culture do your thing' scribed underneath. I get massacred for using words like scribed. I'm too laboured a writer. Or I'm too brusque. I'm too noisy. I'm too cautious. My vocab is in the gutter. The book is left on the shelf like a curio. It's a novelty shrunken head, forgettable for all but the original owner. I become synonymous with Mondays, the worst day of the week, but my book somehow makes Mondays even shoddier. Out of the blue Kate Moss says I'm worse than the easyJet pilot she called a basic bitch. The celebrities pile in. Gordon Ramsay, a man who once said he would electrocute his children if they became vegetarians, calls me a six-foot turkey. I bring out the vitriol in the kindest of stars. Oprah threatens to dangle me over the balcony like Michael Jackson's son. Things reach fever pitch when Lena Dunham says she feels sorry for me but misspells my name and Jon Ronson tweets that I should be scalped. So you've been publicly shaved. The book is translated into Braille solely to exfoliate people's callused feet. 'Ravening' is added to the Oxford English Dictionary, defined as 'writing a shit book'. Tabloid hacks delve into my past and reveal I've been counting my age in Geri Halliwell years and I'm not even half-Jamaican. Piers Morgan calls me Ja-fake-an.

Book people will of course hate the thing, pulling apart my janky prose and grammar. My one-liners fall flat like Christina Aguilera at the Grammys. The *Paris Review* sucker-punches the book as 'a tale told by an idiot, full of sound and fury, signifying nothing'. This hurts me more than the time my mum shut my fingers in the car door in south

London. The *Guardian* blocks me. The *New Yorker* ghosts me. Radio 4 holds a minute's silence rather than platform me. Diet Prada runs a week-long campaign comparing my writing to other writers who've made better points about identical subjects. *Private Eye* has nothing to satirise. For the first time in history the Booker committee decides to award a prize for the *worst* book published this year. Guess who wins? Somebody somehow hacks my Google search history and the world knows how often I investigate eyebag surgery and patterned shorts and synonyms for 'amazing'. The shame is deafening. Charlie Brooker calls my book laughable. Zadie Smith calls me a twat. David Sedaris calls me literary roadkill. Despite this, I refuse to believe the book is shit, such is the ego of a man who's survived. I will die on this hill (the hill being unsold copies of the book).

Back in reality I type onward, telling myself you only have to write the first draft of your first book once. Perhaps I'll look back on this time and laugh, like the time I shat myself in the park on the way to work. Slowly I take more breaks. The world outside the space between my nose and the screen bleeds back in. I loosen the screws on my time-table and word-count. I turn the internet back on. I go to Egypt and I don't write a word and the sky doesn't come crashing down. I watch *Bring It On* in the bath. I bleach the loos and feel a genuine sense of calm but I don't bother with the sinks because it's a faff. I feed my cat M&S smoked salmon. I stop thinking about the book all the time, and the strikethrough of my anxiety Morse codes into intermittent dots and dashes. I decide whatever the outcome I'll always be tall. I write a chapter about being tall. It pretty much writes itself. I watch *Leon* for the first time. I read digestible fashion clickbait which should be forgettable but I find myself thinking, 'I'd better be reincarnated as a French woman, so help me God.' I rewatch the *Blackfish* documentary and think, 'It could be worse, I could get murdered by a killer whale in front of a bunch of kids.' Perhaps I'll be revered in retrospect like Van Gogh or Robbie and Kylie doing 'Kids': not respected enough at the time, but post-reactively iconic. Along with my mood, my prose loosens up like it's taken stool softeners. My coach suggests I write my own eulogy, which I roll my eyes at but it helps because it's all big-picture, blue-sky thinking. I've decided it's bad taste to have my corpse Dita von Teese-floating in a giant novelty martini glass at my funeral, so I want to be dressed in my going-out top and Gucci clogs and burned like a Viking on a pyre of my own belligerence. That would suit me just fine.

Emails

I know it's a humblebrag to say I get a lot of emails and I don't care. I get a lot of emails. I get so many that I now open them to check for urgency and mark them as 'unread', an action I'd like to adopt when I'm being cranky with my husband. *Your washing's been on the radiator for three days.* Mark as 'unsaid'.

An email is always critical for the sender. Falsely flagged as hostage-situation urgent. Only a handful of these inbox delights ever need immediate attention. Technology and productivity have collided, creating a Wild West shootout of hyper-efficiency, where every cowboy touchtypes in bullet time and shoots off a round of emails. Recent etiquette decrees that those on the receiving end must apologise for not replying instantaneously. 'Sorry for the three-minute delay in getting back to you …' Any reply outside of a few hours is insulting and you deserve to be hexed or to lose a finger like the woman in *The Piano*, clacketting away at your keyboard for eternity. If you reply to an email outside of twenty-four hours, the email doesn't even exist, it just turns to foam on the waves like Hans Christian Andersen's Little Mermaid when she can't pull the prince. Rapid-retort emails are the boarding school biscuit game, everyone bashing away trying to get their response out as quickly as possible. Efficiency culture makes us demand things harder, better, faster and stronger, with no margin for error. For all correspondence, we expect the laser precision of a surgeon's knife and the professional finish of a wedding cake.

My fingers automatically type hollow platitudes that keep colleagues and suppliers lubed for the working day. I've lost count of the number of times I've replied 'Amazing!' when the work is adequate. Amazing! keeps the wheels turning. There are more amazing words for Amazing! – Stunning!, Superb!, Magnificent! – but they reek of motivational speaker. Using superior words can make you sound like a nervous Carol Vorderman on a first date with a jittery bag of consonants. Too thesaurus. Too composed. People can smell the bullshit. But Amazing! is timeless and suggests an emotional exertion that isn't really there. Like blue jeans, Amazing! never goes out of style. Like sex, Amazing! is good as long as you're getting it. Amazing! is the bread on a shit sandwich of getting your own way. Pop an Amazing! into an unflinchingly direct command and people think they're helping you out rather than following an order. When your life flashes before your eyes as you die you mainly see instances of the regret and pain you have caused others, but you also see the people whose days were Wonderbra-lifted by a well-placed Amazing!

I've read that flowery emails with too many platitudes are less effective, and that women use this more apologetic lexicon, whereas men just say what they want. In a bid to be assertive I eradicated shriek language from my prose, taking my email tone from giddy teenager in love ('Amazing! Raven xx') to the intensely militant guy in *Full Metal Jacket* ('I need this immediately, as per my last email'). Taking the sweetness out of the emails dropped the blood sugar, and made people feel like I was having a pop. I could almost hear them paralysed at the computer as they received the command, and then scurrying about like frightened church mice. I sort of enjoyed it at a dictator level, but even my inflated sense of self has a boundary. Colleagues felt stressed and inadequate, like me when I lost my virginity. Nobody wants the feeling of deflowerment every time they get an email. Amazing!s were reinstated like a hymen.

Most email communication is superfluous – anything truly urgent happens on the phone, or in the hay-fevered cross-pollination of a conference call, multiple voices and three-second time delays creating an apocalyptic hellfire like when the Ghostbusters crossed the energy streams. You don't email 999. You don't email a boiling pan of water off the stove. Britney didn't email her hair off. Emails are never truly urgent.

Things that are urgent: towels when you get out the bath; chinese food when you're hungover; diet Coke when you're thirsty; Jesus's cross at the crucifixion, or a coffin at a normal funeral; mini quiches at a wake; butter on a jacket potato the moment it comes out of the oven; extra security protocols in action films when people think they have enough security protocols; unlimited patience at Heathrow Terminal 5; Advil PM on a long-haul flight; and Toblerones from duty free. A Starbucks bathroom is urgent when you need to piss. As is masturbation before you sit at a computer all day. Sex when you're horny is an immediate need. Though not having sex immediately is its own thing too. I can convince myself I urgently need more vitamin supplements or new pants, but I'm aware that's just my consumerism talking. I don't want to sound like an emotional wellness coach, but we urgently need friends when we're sad. I'll go all-out and say cake when you're sad, too. And kittens when you're at rock bottom. You need money when you're broke. Or family heirlooms to hock. Or the balls to cat-burgle a stately home, or to Anna Nicole Smith an older man. You urgently need to watch *Antiques Roadshow* if you feel even the slightest bit depressed. It always helps.

What's never urgent is an email. The vibration of a notification is an ambush, striking at any time to jolt you out of the task that had your attention. Notifications can swirl and engulf you like the bees that killed Macaulay in *My Girl*. Endless connectivity is the plague of our century. Ring-a-ring of roses, a pocket full of WeTansfer notifications and breaking news alerts and calendar reminders and the family WhatsApp group. Alerts build in a crescendo that floods all of your senses like a bad case of food poisoning. And we secretly get off on it. We're being alerted to our own sense of importance and need for attention. We welcome the false adoration. It's more than a dopamine hit. The closest thing to an orgasm is turning your phone on after a long flight and flooding the basement with notification vibrations. A reminder that people know you exist. It fortifies our sense of importance. We've convinced ourselves we need to be constantly connected, like those heinous couples on Oxford Street who would rather clothesline you than let go of each other's sodding hands. This is the Braxton Hicks of intimacy. Connectivity making us feel connected, responding to notifications, not people. A false idol of togetherness.

Our egos are bolstered by notice-me-fications, and reinforced by being busy. The culture of being busy isn't a new idea, but I-could-be-doing-more-to-enrich-this-moment is a new pressure. Like a parent at the Tate shoehorning culture into their kid, who just wants to draw. We're trying to find a deeper, multifaceted meaning in every moment. When I was a kid we'd make stained-glass-window biscuits: a shortbread frame with a boiled sweet that would melt in the oven and flood the frame right up to the edges. And that's our new endeavour: trying to fill every day right up to the edges. Like trying to pack a fortnight's clothing into your carry-on. We're adding depth, adding texture. Texture is the right word because it's not about doing more stuff, it's about each life experience having a deeper colour and a coarser consistency, and meaning more because of these things. Like a gin and tonic, but the gin is made by artisanal West Country virgins and the tonic is the expensive stuff from Waitrose.

The lemon is Sicilian and cut with that knife we got in Japan, darling, do you remember? Think of life as spaff of *MasterChef* velouté, and we're all Marco-Pierre White wannabes examining the subtler flavours of the sauce rather than drinking it down like piglets. We're actively seasoning every second we're awake. In any moment's respite from our densely-packed milliseconds we consult our to-do list, the modern prophet for structuring our time.

To-do lists are basically notes we write to ourselves that remind us we exist and have purpose. A list of obstacles that cleverly distracts us from the realisation that regular meditation won't scientifically let us leapfrog death. The humble to-do list keeps existential worries at bay. A to-do list is a breezy nursery rhyme of irrelevant tiny tasks, the lightest of gestures, that keep things ticking forward: *Pick up dry cleaning. Put down my phone. Hydrate.* Trivialities maketh the to-do, as grandiose statements are left for rom-coms when people refuse to forever hold their peace at a wedding. These are things to-do, and when they're to-done we add more. An infinite scroll of distraction, like when you need to leave for work but you can't resist the constant refresh of your news feed. To-do lists represent an evolving, inescapable validation of how we spend our time. The fetish of being so busy we can't stop to think about mortality, every instant of the day chronically stuffed to the brim like a *foie gras* goose. We're choosing to be forever occupied, like a toilet at a house party.

Hotel, Motel, Holiday Thin

There are so many songs about summer the other seasons get jealous. Luckily climate change is a great leveller, and when it's finished we'll have a forever nuclear winter and no seasons at all. In the meantime we can listen to 'Summer Holiday' and get excited for a vacation, no more climate-change worries for a week or two. Saying you love to holiday in Britain is a lie and you deserve to get mad-cow disease. Going on holiday never, ever involves driving down the M25 with all your stuff packed tight in the boot like Stan's girlfriend in 'Stan', your only respite eating the sad, ulcerous motorway food that's been reheated at the back of a garage followed by the empty calories of a Toffee Crisp. Somebody's always crushed into the back seat with their knees by their ears pretending to be jovial. Inevitably a Fathers for Justice guy dressed as Batman blocks the dual carriageway to protest a court order. Hours pass. You piss in a layby. This is not a holiday.

Board the plane without thinking of the carbon foot-print, and join the annual tradition of Brits abroad.

Shakespeare would have loved the ease of an easyJet out of Stansted, penning sonnets and a tragedy or two. Maybe even a Luton haiku. Holidays are important because they heal wounds and knit bone. The bumps and scrapes of daily life are cured, like Jesus and the lepers. Room service is couples therapy. Breakfasting on beer is CBT. Reading a beach thriller is deep psychoanalysis. When everybody is spending in euros your family becomes like the von Trapps, all matching outfits and sing-alongs. Bridge over troubled daughter. Your pent-up aunt is a breeze. Citronella is an aphrodisiac, and it's clinically proven you have better orgasms by the sea. Feta is a superfood. So is ouzo. There are no drawbacks to being away.

Summer is all about deliberate emptiness. Vacations are Dalí landscapes with all the clocks melted, but there's an open bar so you can drink rum and spend a day warm on the sand. In a lifetime of hyper-erranding, a scheduled period for us to go fallow is a must. Beached interludes see us unchained from the shackles of to-do. Just one day out of life. Time with nothing in it, like Oliver Twist's pockets, lolling on a sunlounger in the hourless vacuum in a flask between the tea and your hand. Rest and sleep deep, like the blackout void you had at the staff party sponsored by a tequila brand. Commit for a week, maybe two, just until my skin turns brown then I'm coming back to you.

Mini-breaks are not holidays. They're the crippled boy from 'The Pied Piper of Hamelin' who isn't allowed into the cave of *real* travellers. Mini-breaks are person number three in the human centipede of travel. If travel is a trifle, mini-breaks are in the basement, below the sponge fingers at street level – gelatine from a cow's hoof, maybe. Mini-breaks take you in and out of a city in two minutes, like teenage intercourse. The pace is stressful, more stressful than all the tabs currently open on my computer. Mini-breaks are just the tip, like when straight men sleep with other men. I bite my thumb at mini-breaks. Looking into my crystal ball I can see your mini-break's future: dashing about like *Supermarket Sweep*. Smelling stressed because you are. A cultural hit list, *Sophie's Choice*-ing between the modern art museum and the Sistine Chapel. A rip-off gondola. A rip-off rickshaw. One bite of gelato. A star turn at the Acropolis. A single finger in the Bocca della Verità. Thirty-six hours later you're mini-broken on the tarmac back at Gatwick. Shakespeare's sonnet still a first draft. Mini-break people are the kind of people who think a guy who caught their eye once on the tube is in love with them and then put an ad in the paper trying to find him again. They pen little poems about that fleeting moment for the rest of their lives. The kind of people who believe in short-term, showy romance and buy their girlfriend roses while she waits for them to propose. People who say they get their 'smellies from Boots'. Basic couples dragging their basic luggage across the globe adhering to the artificial signifiers of love.

I hate mini-breaks but I'm also addicted to mini-breaks. They're shit, but my God they're convenient. They're like countershock from a defibrillator when your pulse stutters.

A daytripper global citizen. Venice is literally sinking under the weight of us, but we engage in a personal fallacy: *I'm not part of the problem, I'm not like these other tourists, when I'm here I'm having a unique time, I'm having my own personal cultural experience. I'm not a mini-breaker, I'm a big breaker in a condensed timeframe.* We all want to see the world, but none of us want to leave our creature comforts behind. I'm happy to go halfway round the globe, but I won't give up my San Pellegrino. A cavalier romp on the high seas full of mystery and adventure please, but with a vegan option at dinner. Scott of the Antarctic but comfortable hotel slippers. Indiana Jones and a hot shower. I want the pretence of quill-writing extended witticisms by candlelight, but in reality I immediately go into meltdown if Google Maps can't find me in three seconds.

It's hard to beat a city by the sea. Cities by the sea are like theme parks where you're tall enough for all the rides, freer than their landlocked counterparts, which sprawl ever outwards like a self-levelling screed. You get the metropolis and the marine in one mouthful. Barcelona hits the sea. Manhattan hits the rivers. Rules help control the fun, but there's always something naughty about the nautical.

Getting away from it all has a familiar formula. Booking a holiday is a rain dance for more work. A festival of burnout before you're out of office. The moment you book your vacation your workload quadruples, constipating in a bottleneck. Usual hassles will need more hustle. You'll have missed an initial on a contract and be embroiled in the

Puccinian saga of re-signing and rescanning. You'll spend hours on the phone because you did something really bad to a Virgin Media representative in a previous life. Every meeting you take will be commandeered by a Bob Geldof character on a forty-five-minute tangent about Africa, and you cannot morally interrupt an Africa tangent. Your side-lover becomes irrationally demanding, begging to take you to *Madam Butterfly* and boiling your kid's bunny. You start to receive threatening handwritten letters from the guy you thought you killed on the road after drinking heavily at your graduation party last summer. He has a hook for a hand. All of this you will juggle alongside booking hotel reservations, airport transfers, internal flights, the yellow-fever jab, the ever-so-romantic love in the time of cholera jab, the cult classic rabies jab, passports, travel visas, insurance, additional phone data, insect repellent, miniature shampoo, maps in English, maps in Arabic. Trust me on the sunscreen. Don't forget your toothbrush. Don't forget your plug adapter. Don't forget your plug adapter. Don't forget your plug adapter.

This overabundance of work can make you pre-holiday sick, but exhaustion is the price for escaping, an evacuee of regular employment. You earn your leave by running on pure adrenalin and repeating to yourself, 'I'll sleep on the plane, I'll sleep on the plane.' You need to be dead-body-tired to feel you've earned the trip, otherwise you're an indulgent self-serving monster, one step away from women who lunch. Don't slog hard enough and the undercurrent of opulence will drown you. Your body will wash up on a beach of gold bullion, rubies foaming at your mouth. You don't deserve a life of all play and no work and shuffling your kids off to boarding school like Baroness von Schraeder. Your life will be brunch-time golf and lunch-time facials and three-martini afternoons. All the scenes on *Mad Men* when they're not at the office. Vacationing is your self-care dialled up to eleven, like when Madonna started Wellness with Kabbalah. But you can't be all work and no play, it's biased. You're yin with no yang. Fish without chips. Sandpaper with no rough side. You're one Chuckle Brother. A single Olsen. I don't want to sound dramatic, but after a particularly savage bout of pre-holiday work I developed what I'm certain was either pneumonia or lung cancer or both (I was too scared to Google my symptoms). Before a transatlantic flight I downed a depressingly gendered 'ManFlu Shot' at Heathrow. I do not say this lightly, but it saved my life. After the fish course, I slept deeply for seven hours and sprang into JFK like Tigger on six espressos. It would have saved hours if they'd sent a Manflu Hot or Shot after the Thai boys in the cave from the get-go.

It's glorious to swap the rat race for a queue at the ice-cream van, but the biggest holiday taboo is a winter body on a summer beach. You must get in shape by any means necessary. 'In shape' means you but a dress size smaller, or with more muscly arms, or just after the stomach flu. The 'in-shape' regime begins months before the vacation, as leisurely as the poo you have when nobody else is home because you have time on your side. You will simply eat less and move more. Part of the problem with eating sublimely all day – quinoa porridge and a light lunch of carrot tops – means you're clucking for a pint of lard when you get home. Your naughty inner toddler wants ice cream for dinner, like the French aristocracy in *Les Misérables*. I creamed a cream. You allow this gastronomic transgression because the holiday is weeks away, but you begin to panic as take-off looms closer. Will you fit through the departures gate? You want a hot body? You better work bench. You hit the gym hard. You write *Hotel, motel, holiday thin* on Post-its above the treadmill. You survive on laxative tea and egg whites. After all the militant work and a dash to the airport, you break your fast with a takeaway baguette at Luton airport at 6 a.m. *Auf wiedersehen*, Prêt. You 'accidentally' drink the tap water in a grubby restaurant for a restorative bout of diarrhoea.

People get evangelical about the correct way to pack a suitcase, dishing out tips like a Sunday sermon. As with organised religion, your own moral compass is usually enough. Trust only your own instincts. Pack your bag and go. You'll always have too many long-sleeves and not enough pants. A linen suit is dashing, but will never see the light of day. I always pack multiple white T-shirts, because it's not a question of *if* you spill on then, just *when*. I always want to look like I've been on the road a while, and acclimatised to the temperature, rolling from Greek village to Greek village absorbing acquaintances and atmosphere and chatting to really old locals in bars. I want to give off the romantic air of a man of the world, not a two-week tourist, so I need my outfits to appear a little lived-in, but also hardy and practical. Shorts with enough pockets for my compass and penknife and luxury leather wallet. A neckerchief to stop condensation running down my spine. I want to look like the sort of languid person who can play 'Nowhere Man' on guitar (I can't), and has a lot of stories to tell (I don't), with a girl in every port (nope). He smokes rollups. He nurses half a beer. I don't wear shorts because it's sunny, I wear them because of Ernest Hemingway in Cuba, Italian beaches with Picasso, and Howard Carter when he discovered Tutankhamun. Or the sexy police chief from *Jaws*. A Myspace top eight of men's legs traversing the globe. I want to be an archaeologist, not a holidaymaker; a zookeeper, not a backpacker. To have a purpose beyond touristing and tanning. I don't dress for mai tais at Soho House. I honestly don't. I don't dress to lob coins in the Trevi Fountain or to pretend to push the Tower of Pisa over. I nod to historic pioneers and grafting ancestors and the ever-so-problematic colonialists. This is my truth. When I travel I also want the bulky, irritating thirties luggage that takes several bellboys to manoeuvre to your suite, and I want someone else I employ to quietly slip them a crisp note for their troubles. A monogrammed trunk is the final boss of vacation packing, but it's a bugger to lift. I love saying I'm low-maintenance and then packing a month's worth of skincare into a leather weekender for an overnight stay thirty-five minutes from my house. I wish I knew how to quit you, Retinol.

Some people want to fill the world with silly little love songs. These people don't get cheap flights out of Luton at 4 a.m. You need to dull the noise. The first thing I do when I get to an airport is head to that fishy rotunda of high stools and order white wine. It's always near the diminutive Fortnum's. The wine is expensive and unnecessary, which is the exact mood of any vacation. I sip Sancerre until I'm rehabilitated from the systematic abuse of check-in and security. The first thing I do on the plane is order a bloody mary. I don't like them, but that's beside the point. People who drink bloody marys are default dashing fifties bachelors. I read that the Queen drinks a gin and Dubonnet before lunch, a glass of wine with her lunch, and a glass of champagne before bed, and I follow this triptych hourly as I fly. After this concoction of booze you have a wonderful flight, even in the middle seat with the worst turbulence. Wherever I am in the royal booze cycle I always down a glass of champagne before landing. At the hotel I order a martini as dry as my face when I'm fake-crying to get out of trouble. With a twist. Olives on the side. Not crisps. I sleep till noon the next day.

I always say you're not on holiday until you've got drunk twice and had sex twice. The way you achieve this is *carte blanche*. People get horny in prickly heat. One cousin will emerge from a cloud of Impulse with newly budded breasts and you'll all pretend you haven't noticed. After you've done all your selfies for the day, spritz your facial mist and lie back and think of nothing. Read whatever you want, too. The trashier the better. When Amazoning holiday reads copy Rihanna singles and alternate between nuanced, emotional hard-hitters and banging classics. A dishevelled, carefully undone mood permeates each sunlit second. Like a bag of chips, the perfect beach hair has just the right amount of salt. You get butterflies in the stomach from too much heat. The smell of Piz Buin mixes with Malibu, blowing through the jasmine of your mind. Your face hurts from smiling. You're *that* person. You pat aloe vera on peeling shoulders under a paper-thin top you Febreze every night. Batman's utility belt, but full of suntan lotion and aftersun. Swimming naked. Dining in jelly shoes. Sex is great, but have you ever had three ouzos in a taverna? You'll have a series of crushes on inappropriate waiting staff. By all means shag the kitchen porter if you can shake the image of where his hands have been. You momentarily commit to single-use everything – napkins, straws, lovers. Non-stop daiquiris. Non-stop dancing. Non-stop dick. Catching crabs is a thrilling game of jeopardy, rather than a worry. Sand gets into every nook and cranny and you just laugh. You get sick on the coach from too many windy roads.

You'll mainly eat crisps. The occasional salad. Three different varieties of crisp in a bowl *is* a type of salad. But when you travel it's imperative to visit the first McDonald's you see and sample the local delicacies. The one in the airport doesn't count. In Japan I detoured a press trip to a

Shinjuku Maccy Ds for a 4 a.m. tasting menu. The green Fanta was excellent, a supernatural gunge colour signalling how desperately bad for you it must be. A tonic for my barbed-wire throat after refusing the microphone at karaoke. The giant spicy chicken nugget was more of a question than an answer, essentially a deep-fried disc of salted enigma that still perplexes. But the carbonara fries changed our collective lives. Carbonara fries immediately feel like a bad idea, like the people still wearing pun versions of Make America Great Again hats. Carbonara fries doesn't even sound Japanese, does it? But there comes a point in every young man's life when he must rethink all he holds to be true. Bittersweet and strange, finding you can change, learning you were wrong. Our preconceptions of carbonara fries: an unnecessary union, defamation of two sublime and independent dishes. A cut and shut car. A bootleg, flying in the face of God. But in this instance God is Nigella Lawson and she's silently sobbing. Lo! Behold! the greatest dish on the planet. The 'chefs' at McDonald's have reinvented the wheel. On first taste carbonara fries assault your very humanness. An explosion in the mouth like throwing water on a chip-fat fire. An immense salty jizz of translucent sauce fists great punches of parmesan into your gullet like an overzealous lover grabbing you by the throat when the safe word is 'more parmesan'. It's just the most needlessly cheesy foghorn, blasting cheese down your chest into your guts and soggy in the wrong places like drunk sex. The sauce is stabbed through with heroic shards of bacon like angry bees swarming half a grapefruit but the grapefruit is a potato cut into matchsticks and fried to perfection. We finished the lot humming 'Food, Glorious Food', and we Ubered back to our hotel, happy as pigs in shit (that were gladly sacrificed to become the bacon on carbonara fries).

At some point you have to come home from vacation, because you miss your clean white linen and your fancy French cologne. Head back to the absurdities of everyday life and the sinkhole of adult responsibilities (similar to kids' responsibilities if they had to pay taxes). But before you board easysqueezyJet you need to deliver the ultimate humblebrag: a postcard. Postcards, the worst invention known to humanity. Worse than the atomic bomb or Chewits or belly shots. There are two types of postcard. First there are the picturesque twee tableaus of model villages sent by undersexed Wes Anderson Oxford alumni whose specialist subject on *Mastermind* is Hogwarts. The second type of postcard is the chunkily sexual teenage-boy-who's-never-seen-tits-in-the-flesh innuendo postcard – an archipelago of women's arses in neon thongs, men basking in the shade of an obese woman, a man's penis wearing sunglasses. To be honest, I sort of love those unwoke postcards. Feel free to send me those, but if you send me a Wes Anderson postcard may someone with the flu lick your Ryanair tray table. You do not wish I was there. You are atoning for your own enjoyment. Sorry to be *that guy*, but have you ever read a postcard that stayed with you after ten minutes? Be honest. I don't mean a MoMA postcard with compact-but-touching emotive script. I mean a list of taverns and tourist traps. Again, sorry to be *that guy*, but can you think of a single postcard you've been sent that touched you? A dramatic postcard? Or an arresting one? A postcard so illuminating and eye-catching and staggeringly surprising that it inspired awe? A transcendent postcard, both humbling and sensational? Impressive in its subtlety, yet awe-inspiring in its nuanced articulation? A postcard that reminded you how great it is to be alive, like the Scrooge ghosts or that lumpectomy that came back benign?

The problem is, no matter how small your handwriting, postcards are only ever a tiny morsel of the full trip experience. Thirty degrees of the 360. You only ever get a manageable highlights reel, like GCSE Bitesize. The bare bones that basically say 'Ate stuff, saw stuff.' And it's incredibly hard to escape the latent boast or the ingrained gloat in such a short form. Teensy bits of paper lack depth. There's a reason the Ten Commandments weren't written on A5. There's a reason we don't protest with postage stamps. Postcards are the preserve of a bygone era, when people couldn't show off their lives on Instagram. We're so digital now that seeing someone's handwriting is like seeing their nutsack. Their signature has a perverse intimacy. Postcarding is a dying art, like falconry or plumbing, because we're conditioned to expect more from short-form content. It's difficult to read something short that isn't an instant-laugh meme or doesn't want you to buy something. We'll be sorry in the future when all the digital data gets wiped by the Rihanna hacker in *Ocean's 8*. The digital world will disappear, the Cloud will disperse. We'll clutch our postcards to our chests and fondly caress them. We'll dig out the Yellow Pages and meet in person. Our attention spans and short-term memories will come back.

Until then, wear white to show off your radiation burn while the Macarena plays softly on piano.

Marathon Love

When you first meet someone it's a like a starter's pistol going off. Bang bang he shot me down. The energy is electric. A rush, a surge, a sprint forward. You start pelting headlong like a blinkered horse. Running like a tap. Running like Obama for president. Running like clockwork towards an unknown finish line. Each little spark of discovery igniting more passion. Pining for their newness, their novelty. Scientists say it's all projection – that we see mainly what we want to see, mixed with a few matching pheromones, like the Sorting Hat put you both in Hufflepuff and you both wear CK One. A biological fuckery. Truffle pigs sniffing each other out like gourmet fungus. But honestly, who cares about the science? Once you get the scent you tear downhill, risking a nosedive that will mash your front teeth onto the pavement. Race through the halcyon opening numbers. First date, first kiss, first finger. Luck be a lady every night. When you're a gay you get the added frisson of who will pay for dinner and who will top. It's a thrill ride, like a ghost train with manageable scares because it's not too serious yet. You're not all the way *committed*. It's a cushioned kamikaze and you're bolstered by the energy of the new. New car, new girl, new ice, new glass. You're whipped into a sandstorm frenzy, never waiting long enough for the dust to settle, tearing forward like pingpong balls in the updraught. Venice is for lovers, so you go for the weekend. Let's punt in Oxford. A weekend in the Lakes. Did my heart not love till Slough? Paris in the spring? And flowers are brilliant. *Une douzaine de roses, s'il vous plaît.*

The aggressive romancing you do to snare a partner is textbook and contrived and naff. That's all part of the fun, because in the early days of a love affair, in *romcom world*, the impossible is made possible. The workaholic boss ends up with the office temp. The ugly duckling emerges from behind her glasses and bags the coolest guy in school. The nerd gets the girl. Life before was flat, but love reinflates your tyre on the side of a dual carriageway. Falling in love is brilliant. You are Jake Gyllenhaal coming back down the mountain after getting his cheeks clapped by Heath Ledger. Beaming like the Cheshire cat. It's like when your Instagram post is doing numbers. You manically sprint through this phase, pausing only for a Lucozade Sport and hand jobs. You forget simple things because your head is full of him. Or her. You don't keep up with the current political hell (there's always some). You run out of food at home. You have sex in daylight, arrive at events late and just-showered. You throw out compliments like the guy feeding penguins fish at London Zoo. Turtledoves working out how to spend

Christmas. Their cute foibles are still cute. The word prenup just a whisper.

Fall in love. Stay in love. These are the rules of life. There's very little grey area. No margin for error. Do not get left on the shelf. Do no old maid. Do not Grey Gardens. Fall in love, stay in love. The mantra is a maypole for your entire existence that all the other ribbons plait around. I will fall in love and the rest will fall into place. It's fantastic to become incredibly successful at a job you love and eat the food you love and see the world. But all that is noise outside of the fall-in-love mantra, an unmoving maypole to dance round.

As the first wave of tsunami love subsides you find yourself attached. Tethered. Coupled. Staying in love. That's not a bad thing. But it's not a sprint either. It's more leisurely. A foot taken half off the gas. *Being* in love isn't like falling in love. It's more of an inert gas that forms around you as a couple, and sometimes a few drops of condensation fall. There are glorious months, or even years, when you still posture with money, booking exotic faraway trips and non-invasive beauty treatments. You still get on famously. The falling in love part tends to take your mind off everything else, but real life starts to ebb back in as time passes. Your heart rate de-escalating after intercourse, lying in the dark, remembering that email unsent in drafts.

I need to go back in time before we go forward in this piece. If you want my future, forget my past. In retrospect, all the young dudes I slept with in my youth were stepping stones en route to my husband, but I didn't know that so I mourned each of them like those old women on Kos in all black. My lovers were a series of false starts, a lengthy warm-up. None of them were tonics. These guys were mouthfuls of dry gin and bitter lemon. We're all, I think, attracted to a danger of sorts when we're young. There's something about the invincibility of youth that makes us desire instability, the destabilising rock of rock 'n' roll. We love the idea that musicians act insane offstage. That their creativity comes from eccentricity, some brain alchemy that distinguishes a true creative from mere mortals. Michael Jackson, David Bowie, Madonna. All somehow other. All somehow flawed (sometimes fatally), a fissure running down the middle of their excellence. We're never satisfied with stable, we want a peculiarity, we want a fault line of danger.

Dating bad boys is a real thrill, there's no denying it. But bad boys grow into bad men. I was magnetically drawn to guys who seemed like they never slept, in tight jeans and billowy seventies blouses under leather jackets, as was the rage. Complete idiots were catnip. Bleeding arrogant two-bob cunts turned my head. The fucking hours I clocked up obsessing over men that didn't fancy me at all. I really should invoice them.

Most relationships start online now, so I always think of those early endeavours as traditional and even more chaotic because every decision was based on gut feeling and adrenalin. Every great love story tells you drama is the key to happiness, but that approach tends to leave you single, with a clapped-out adrenal gland. I dated countless Tybalts we both thought were Romeos. I once dated a kleptomaniac. It was short-lived, on account of his deep, bleeding wound of despair over the death of his sister, clumsily staunched with stolen H&M belts. He's fine now, by the way (I've always been a little bit too self-involved to be a proper 'rescuer'). Another boyfriend was a more sensible choice, but choosing sensibly is in itself doomed, because snuggles in your twenties are not cool, and I wanted to be swept off my feet. Staggeringly, two of my exes ended up together, proving you can re-gift ex-boyfriends like unwanted scented candles. I'm being flippant, because I was properly devastated and it took fucking ages to stop picturing them rutting. My smile is my make-up I wear since my break-up with you. Like the assassin bug that wears the corpses of its victims as armour, these experiences built quite a nice shield to keep me safe. I zipped any signs of vulnerability into my skinny jeans, layered up my blouses, and kept drinking.

There are two types of love. One that makes you cry a lot and feel very alive. The other makes you feel totally safe. Great relationships, in my experience, contain very little drama but still a great deal of feeling. They make for bad telly. Anthony and Cleopatra on *Gogglebox* doesn't quite work. Dating the wrong type of guy is all very thrilling before the coin flips and it becomes incredibly tiring. I was exhausted when I met my husband, and my patience for bullshit was paper-thin. We had just the right amount of dicking about. And he's still the most matter-of-fact person

I know. It's been a full decade since we met on the top deck of the night bus. A ten-year lease. A decade of us. Cut me open and count the rings. I remember being ten years old, so I guess our relationship can legally be arrested and can remember throwing up jelly sweets at Alton Towers. It can be measured in food fads, and the meals I would cook for him regularly and *faux*-casually. The cottage-pie years, the ratatouille years, the meat-zza years (revolting, but I was more anti-carbs then).

The cottage pies started about six months into the relationship, when we lived separately and I wanted more of a commitment, and the pies reflected that desire to seal the deal – we once had cottage pie with a cauliflower cheese topping. In one dish. These are the stupid things you do for love when you're in a low-responsibility professional role and can be on the bus home with Waitrose mince by 6 p.m. Nowadays we get a boughie little organic veg box delivered on a Wednesday, which my husband has no idea what to do with. He's from the school of cooking where you buy all the ingredients at the same time to make the meal, which I find infuriating and irksome and desperately attractive. I'm from the significantly more pretentious school of kitchen goddess-ing, where true cooking means being able to rustle some-thing up out of nothing. We always have a stack of eggs, and I believe you can grate pretty much anything into a frittata if you chase it with enough cheese.

I digress. This chapter would never end if I mentioned every time I fell more in love with him, so we'll skip past any more saccharine reminiscing of our particular love sprint. We got married for the only reason gays get married: as a piece of homonormative propaganda to wind up the other gays. Fast-forward from the sprint to the marathon, reality biting so hard as you knuckle down, saving your cash and energy for important life stuff. A cat, maybe, a mortgage, a kid. All the living you do between vacations.

A long-term relationship is like following a very complex Agatha Christie novel, knowing you missed key plot points earlier and they'll come back to haunt you. There are red herrings and false clues, but you don't get the luxury of a library in your house or art deco architraves. You can't skip ahead, there are no spoilers, and you either die on the last page or break up. P.S. When I die my last will and testament is just a schedule to feed the cat and instructions for smuggling my ashes into the meals of my enemies.

Of all the things I ever wanted for my life – marriage, kids, unlimited access to shortbread – I never thought it would be *this much* hard work. I thought you could fire up the engine at university and leave it running all the way to middle age. Keep your head down until retirement. 'My whole life will be a banquet!' I thought. After a hearty breakfast of education I'll take a gap-year palate-cleanser and coast in a fulfilling job until all the pudding at the end. I'd discard healthy eating and exercise just before death. Burn my body in the house like Gilbert Grape's mom. I planned to muddle through the stodgy mains and fudge the edges. But there's been absolutely no fudge since university.

It's like running Charlie's Chocolate Factory without sugar or cocoa solids and having to turn a profit while the stakeholders gather outside with pitchforks and an effigy.

The banquet of my life is not a bad night out at all, but the main course hasn't appeared, so it's all £4 carby sides. My blood sugar's low and the kitchen keeps sending out the same dauphinoise that's somehow both too boring to unconsciously ingest and too rich to stomach. You and your partner sit across from each other, very much at the same table but often eating from different menus, electricity crackling between you. You are in a mood for three days after you use Google to win an argument and find you're wrong (the meaning of architrave, for example). He tells you you look *fine* and you silently seethe for the entirety of July. He sends you a Spotify playlist but he *knows* you're Apple Music. How could he not know that? Does he not know you at all? Is this burning an eternal flame or building up resentment?

This bit in the middle is meant to be the hog-roast years. I thought I'd be on autopilot as I dolloped apple sauce on my baps and asked for more crackling. But this era is majority graft with short breaks when I get drunk enough to briefly forget the exertion. Five or ten years ago everything I wanted only took half a day to achieve. I quit smoking in two hours. I stopped wearing skinny jeans and buying the *Sun*. Now my life is conversely both hyper-slow and hyper-convenient. I can have a meal delivered to the door in thirty minutes, but we can't find a womb to incubate heirs for love nor money (don't get me started on how much that costs). I can get a chin-up new outfit to my door in four hours, but I can't legally move an inconvenient wall in my house that's definitely hollow when I knock on it. All I really want our love to do is to bring out the best in me and in him too. But we also need to save for new floors. And the womb rental. Life gets in the way.

Everything is protracted and repetitive and doesn't move you forward, like Gareth Gates introducing himself on *Pop Idol*. It's like someone is constantly playing the first note of a concerto for two years. Or not even that. It's like when the entire orchestra is playing the same hum note in the warm-up. I just want to hear a few bars of the concerto. When we moved into our *château* I never thought I'd wake up every day in a cold bedroom because no matter how many times I bleed the upstairs radiators the one next to the bed is only ever half full. It courageously gasps out little wheezes of lukewarm air, but they're immediately absorbed into our unvarnished splinter-ridden floor (we have to wear shoes right up to the bed, which is not sexy, let me tell you). The room isn't draughty *per se*, but there are fissures between the window pane and the frame, so sometimes you're hit by a laser-precision dart of cold air, like somebody's blowing on you through a plastic straw. These fissures also let in sound. I hate the foxes on my street keeping me awake all night with their screeching. I'm certain Fantastic Mrs Fox is being penetrated in an orifice she's not accustomed to using that way, which makes a noise like a thousand wet balloons griping at once. And the binmen are just pure noise. Worse than jazz. There's also the Uber driver who regularly stops outside my house to piss in a bottle and throw it into the gutter. I don't have the balls to knock on the window to scare him off like a pigeon. I'd love to shut the world out, but the innards of my house are no sanctuary. There's a matrix of major and minor jobs that need doing before we get to the windows. Here's a verbatim forward from my husband: *Fwd: Our quotation is £695.00 + VAT for the 1 x Party Wall Awards, 1 x Notices and 1 x Condition Schedules.* It's impossible to sprint through an email as dry as this. It's like trying to rollerblade through treacle.

Marathon love is an Eton mess of experiences and emotions – all your meringues get smashed, but they're still edible. Life is random paint-strokes of grievances and appreciations that build the masterpiece of any union. You have to stand back to see the full picture, but close scrutiny shows the work. At the frontline it's a committed slog, the kind of graft you don't write about because it's much easier to mention sprinting off the night bus into each other's arms, or Pancake Day, or anything but the quiet dramalessness of a good marriage. Marathon love is a fractured metatarsal you can still walk on and nobody offers you a splint so you hunker down and try not to kick up an unnecessary fuss. Over the course of a marathon there are good bits, great bits, transcendent moments of fully dilated pleasure, but they're glimpses of grout between slabs of hard graft and patience and trying to be your best self. Relationships are a perpetual Monday night: the pub is uneventful and complaintive and nobody ever calls time. One part of you loves the quiet, the other part of you wants taking to the end of the week already, to the merriment and noise and overstimulation.

Inevitably, a unique knowledge of your partner builds like couture, perfectly tailored to the other person. Partners can be stubborn to the point of self-destruction, like an animal refusing to board Noah's ark. Partners can be disagreeable, like a budget flight. Partners are both the North Star guiding you through all the bullshit, and the bullshit itself growing like damp. Partners are the only people who really know how to push your buttons. Partners are the only people who *should* really know how not to. Partners know the little in-jokes, and can divert the oncoming storm of an argument. Between the sunny spells, resentment can build up like thin layers in a good wok. It doesn't matter what he's cooked tonight, because you can always taste that one forgotten anniversary. Every innocuous comment has micro-subtext. Every fart is Pompeii. Every other gift is the Joni Mitchell CD from *Love Actually*. Somehow marathon love is both super-intense HIIT workouts with no recovery periods, and the quiet, exhausting seasonal nothingness between Christmas and, erm, wow, it's Christmas again. Where did the time go? Why don't we have proper floors yet? Somewhere in the middle of this you ideally smash like the avocados you prepared for lunch, and keep tabs on world events and culture. Keeping your eye on the ball is exhausting. The biggest decision used to be where to have dinner on Friday or when to take a shit without the other person knowing how long you've been gone. (Honestly, nail the shit schedule as early as possible.) Suddenly you have to decide whether your kids' names are too classic or too pretentious, and whether they're going to be organically reared or privately educated.

A long-term relationship is a bit like a Netflix binge: you keep watching each scene, but sometimes you're not fully following the plot. You're committed to seeing out the series, but the drama in front of you maybe doesn't have your full attention. I get the nagging suspicion I'm going to *Gone Girl* my husband because he doesn't appreciate me. My ego needs stroking like a tabby. I want to be noticed the way hardcore Americans stare at you if you don't stand up while their national anthem is playing. Oh, bae can you see by the dawn's early light. Longing to be objectified like the early days. Salad days are manageable, but decades of dauphinoise are tougher. You try and shake a depressing thought: I would happily go to bed on an argument, but I wouldn't miss my skin regime for anything or anyone. Does that mean I care more about my pores than about my husband?

Ten years in and nothing ever goes horribly wrong. And nothing goes stupidly right. Nothing's changed, I still love you. Marathon love is nothing like Elizabeth Bennet and Mr Darcy. It's not Bonnie and Clyde. It's not even Kylie and Jason. It's Saturday at kids' parties as forty toddlers come up on party rings. It's Sundays at Sainsbury's. It's enjoying being apart. It's being together in silence. It's singing at the top of your lungs in the car. It's biting your tongue. It's picking at your feet in broad daylight. Marathon love needs different sustenance from a sprint. It needs the nutrient-rich compost you only get from being agreeable and listening, which sounds easy but isn't. The sprint is always short-lived. Live fast, die young. A marathon takes time. Look how far we've come, my baby.

Croissant

I think of New Year's Eve as amateur night. People who don't drink go out and drink heavily on empty stomachs. Novices cram the bar because they don't know how to get a barman onside to make ordering easy (it's called tipping, Brenda, look it up). They don't know how to manoeuvre their sequin jumpsuit to take a quick piss. Their hair is too big and their shoes are too impractical. They don't know how to pace themselves like a cross-country runner; they sprint as soon as the pistol goes off. They become a chanting football crowd way too early, usually to 'Sweet Caroline'. They loll about, Night Nurse-level drowsy, hours before midnight. They don't know how to drink water or acquire sobering drugs. By 11.30 they've lost their wallets and their minds, sequins rolling out onto the dancefloor, mascara-smeared eyes looking for fireworks. They beg for water like James Franco in *127 Hours*, dried out like cuttlefish husks you find on the beach.

It sounds like I'm only talking about women, but groups of men aren't allowed in anywhere on New Year's Eve.

They're split up into pairs to hunt in fractured packs, trying to friend the doormen of London. They're Tiny Tims outside in the cold, peering through the gap in a blackout blind in the window of a club. Straight men desperately trying to finger straight women on a night out is the greatest propaganda for homosexuality.

All in all, it's a ghastly night. A horrible high-heel hell. The next morning you step over stupored women, splayed like Liberty rugs on the pavement. The streets smell of croissants and vomit, the odour of gentrification.

In a bid to escape the night's brutal frivolities, my husband and I once spent a New Year's Eve on the beach in Mexico, which sounds pretentious and expensive because it was. The trip was a little cultural bump between work gigs. The dress code was all-white, we had sparklers at midnight, and I remember being very drunk and very naked in the sea, which is terrifying. Trudging back to our concrete cabin at 2 a.m. on New Year's Day I felt like Florence Nightingale but with iPhone torches rather than a chic little gas lamp. We'd got stuck talking to a troupe of gay American doctors at dinner, which sounds like a brilliant Tinder match, but they were as dry as a Ryvita on a radiator. Making friends abroad is important. Ideally find an ex-spy, because they have brilliant anecdotes and happily slag off whichever country they're in because they've always travelled for business on somebody else's money. Their loyalty is shot to pieces. We think we found one in Cuba, but I couldn't possibly go into that. He had a bag full of condiments like raspberry vinegar in a country where black pepper has never happened. So suspicious.

Nursing half a coconut at the Mexican beach bar the next day I thought about how you make friends with people, and fretted that I'm terrible at it. I love going to drinks things and meeting new people and being charming and memorable and leaving before I turn back into a pumpkin. I'm less good at long conversations with new people, where you have to actually listen, rather than doing a *listening face* for a spell and then floating away. Usually if you go to a big dinner, you meet someone you click with at the pre-drinks but you're seated six kilometres away from them, with a mid-century screen and several pot plants between you. You didn't know you needed them in your life until today. You want more of them, reopening the app you just closed, but it's too late to bait-and-switch place settings. You spend the rest of the night trying to get back to them, like Marty McFly and 1985. I've long-term clicked with maybe eight people my entire life, but short-term clickage needs to be savoured and cherished like a 99 with a Flake on a summer's day. Enjoy it, but do not expect it to last forever. Move mountains to get back to your clickee, drawn together as you are like Ryan and the other Privates. Stop at nothing. The two of you are steak and béarnaise. Ignore the all-singing, all-dancing French appetisers from *Beauty and the Beast*'s magical kitchen, and politely wrap up conversations like Willy trying to get back to the ocean.

I find the graft of not clicking with people so gruelling. You fit with them like O.J. Simpson's hands in the gloves before he walked to freedom like Nelson Mandela. With unclicked acquaintances the conversation flows like treacle on a completely flat surface on a particularly cold day. You feel every second, the way you've been trying to achieve with daily mindfulness sessions, but each one is agony, dragging like a corpse across a carpet of pure friction. If I'm really not interested in a person, I sometimes find myself burying them in witty anecdotes, right up to the neck like an Aztec human sacrifice. I can lob personal histories out like the necklace at the end of *Titanic*, letting them sink without trace, indifferent to their final resting place. I guess they settle on the person's seabed. I focus on leaving a good impression and leaving good times in my wake. I must sound like the Mad Hatter on speed. Memories light the corners of my mind, but the edges are frayed like Vetements jeans as I wring personal narrations from my damp-towel memory. *I should talk about the time I was cast as a paparazzo in Fergie's 'London Bridge' video. Or mention that I'm getting hypnotised to stop eating Prêt baguettes. I should say there's a film on Goop where* Queer Eye*'s Antoni Porowski and Gwyneth Paltrow competitively make meatloaf like a battle royale of turkey bread. Gwyneth uses panko breadcrumbs, which strikes me as even more Goopy. I once made a 'soup' by putting a jar of sun-dried tomatoes in a blender and it just tasted like sweet oil. I once watched six minutes of* Burlesque *on Netflix that completely skewed my algorithm* *recommendations and now I get singing women suggested on the homescreen. I watched the whole of the first* Sex and the City *film with the Patricia Field styling commentary and she spent twenty minutes describing types of skirts. Sometimes I want my look to be super-minimal Yoko Ono. Sometimes I want my look to be expensive pole dancer but not too much flesh. I once went ice-skating with my mum and her boyfriend and he slipped over and sat on my head. Last year my yoga teacher laid a towel over me in child's pose before touching me because I was so sweaty and I've never shaken the shame. I saw a watercolour of the original Berghain building and I can't stop thinking about penny-farthinging down a cobbled street on poppers. I think of my cat as my beautifully ugly son. There's a secret arrow in the FedEx logo you can never unsee.* Wait, what were you saying? Never mind.

Be warned, fellow party monsters, I do this flash flood of chatter to people I *like* as well. My babble knows no discrim-ination. It's an assault of anecdotes, with micro-breaths for air. If the dear listener does manage to talk I just wait for a gap in the conversation, riffling through my head Filofax. Combing the mind-beach like a lonely guy with a metal detector when the Thames is low. All this while I'm doing the *I'm listening and engaged* face for an appropriate amount of time. It's actually an exact photocopy of the art face I do. It's weird how despite years of training and craft, art appre-ciation essentially boils down to looking at nudes and pretending you're not titillated. Pretending you don't like bums or boobs. If you snigger you're common. Museums and galleries are pin-drop quiet because of the repressed horniness and doused loin fires. Same with nunneries.

Anyway, the *faux*-quizzical *I'm listening* face is an empty gesture, like repeatedly offering thoughts and prayers rather than reforming gun laws. My head is full of unattributed facts, like plaques donated by anonymous donors. The poor unfortunate soul sat next to me must endure the manic outpouring. *The word 'testify' is based on the Ancient Roman practice of making men swear on their testicles in court. A bra manufacturer made Neil Armstrong's spacesuit, so six hundred million people tuned in to watch him walk on the moon in a bra. Armstrong couldn't cry during the walk because tears can't flow in zero gravity, (if that's not a metaphor for toxic masculinity I don't know what is). Women blink nearly twice as often as men but I don't know why. The phrase 'rule of thumb' is derived from an English law that you couldn't beat your wife with anything wider than your thumb. Jellyfish are 95 per cent water. Leonardo da Vinci invented scissors. Babies are born without kneecaps (this is my favourite thing to tell new mums).*

I do this at lunches too, pretending to listen, wanting to speak. Lunch is the best meal of the day because you're at your least tired and cranky and you have the whole afternoon to catch up on the work you didn't do in the morning because you were reading the Lifestyle pages of the *Guardian*. Taking a long lunch makes you feel important, like you work in an office where someone else shoulders responsibility for the running of things while you're out wining and dining and sixty-nining. Your absence is your mystery.

People think you're making shit happen: closing the big deal or getting the important contract signed. People assume you're working at level 10, and have secret meetings about your potential burnout. In reality you're functioning at a 4, relaxed but unsteady. Absence is your cloak of invisibility. You can't disciplinary-hearing a ghost.

People don't really drink wine at lunch, it makes you look a bit louche. Red wine makes you look gouty, like a sitting prince who doesn't have a war to fill his time with. The sitting prince is rotting inside, his stomach swollen with red meat and potatoes and *petits fours*. Not a single item of fruit or veg, but maybe some of those mirage pieces of painted fruit that are actually meat. White wine is called lady petrol, which is so sexist you should hard pass on vaginal grounds. Feminists don't touch Chablis. Wine also makes you skinny fat: when you look reasonable but all your arteries are strangled with sugary tissue. Your exterior is the Taj Mahal but the interior's been converted into dingy bedsits. Rosé got rebranded as brosé and never really recovered because even bros have standards. It was funny when the all the rosé ran out in the Hamptons, but only because we love to see rich people suffer – watching rich people in crisis is a national sport much like purging your suppressed emotions at the football. A boozy lunch is the bastion of a bygone era when you could get ahead if you had the right parents and could afford to intern for half a century before getting your entry-level job. Watching people who cheated the system fail makes us smile.

Back at lunch, if someone offers you wine it's rude to say no but fake a grape allergy and order a martini. Like Evian facial spray, martinis got me feeling rich. Order one of each pudding and let the afternoon roll out. Hit vibrate and silence the lambs back in the office. Imagine you're in *Mad Men* and you didn't promise to swing by Sainsbury's for cat food on the way home tonight. Pretend you have a tie clip and murmur things about 'Nam as you fondle an olive. Get misty eyes as you remember old comrades. Martinis are an afternoon in themselves, so prepare for the long haul. Wine is benign, but martinis are a slippery slope with a steep incline and you're Bambi in rollerblades. Their blatant fuck-it-ness quickly turns you inwards. Even the most stealthy of drinkers can have difficulties disappearing martinis at lunchtime. It can leave you like the aforementioned New Year's Eve lushes, rolling back into your office at 4 p.m. covered in croissants and vomit. That disciplinary hearing becomes less of a theory.

I really do love a chat. When I meet new people I love the scent of the chase, the pheromones of interest they give off. Metaphorically sniffing each other's bums like dogs. The silent sussing out you do while you small-talk and glance at them when they're not looking. Sizing them up. I somehow can't be arsed to follow up on every single thing they say, but I think that makes a better convo. I insert myself into their transmission, so not every sentence gets completely finished. That sounds annoying, and it might well be. My anecdotes just pour out, like Niagara Falls or New Year's vomit on the

— 61 —

pavement. Grab a waterproof poncho. Oops I said something about myself again. I see the clues a conversation is ready to develop like a string of negatives, but I can't stop expressing myself to engage with them properly. I'm great at interviews because I love a chat, not because I ask loads of questions. I'm always caught in the slipstream of the conversation rather than steering it.

I'm genuinely driven by the newness of new people, but there's a laziness to my curiosity in a way that wouldn't cut it on the *Today* programme. I don't think great conversationalists think that many steps ahead. I don't think I'm the kind of newspaper hack who would eventually reveal Batman's identity, though Bruce Wayne might let it slip as we share New Year's plans. April O'Neil following a giant rat into the sewers for a story is all well and good, but I can tell you where Splinter gets his fur trimmed. While social situations are about letting go, proper investigation is all about holding on. Great conversation is two people letting go and falling together without worrying about the ground approaching. It takes energy to stay as sharp as a Savile Row suit when you chat. It's a phenomenal skill I'm honing. But nowadays I always think of great questions when I'm in the Uber home. I say things to my husband like 'She was fun,' and he'll ask me what her job was and I won't have a clue. Literally no idea. While I ponder the etiquette of a follow-up conversation in letter form, I crank open the window and inhale the aroma of croissants.

The Fridge

You can tell a lot about someone from the contents of their fridge. As soon as your one-night stand falls asleep, open the guy's fridge and read the interior like the palm of a hand. Personality traits line every shelf, more revealing than hacking his phone. A guy with normal dairy yoghurt is dateable, but almond milk always spells danger. At first it's all laughter and chickpeas and standing at the finish line with a foil blanket while he runs a half-marathon. He's fit but not too fit, a meaty torso forged from veganism. But before you know it he's slowly controlling your intake of dairy, eroding your confidence in double cream and undermining your burrata starter. You'll divorce three years later in a flurry of tofu on Pancake Day. Flash-forward to you sobbing alone in a bedsit clutching a tiny cube of Edam, knowing you want it but still a prisoner of his coercive veganism. If your one-night stand has bacon and eggs in the fridge, don't be afraid to catch feels. The next two years are an audition for marriage, a rollercoaster of obligatory sexist drivel and gendered habits. Sneak back into bed and feel his boner in the small of your back. Engage in the prehistoric dating practices that still underpin modern love. Massage his ego. Massage his feet. Massage his mediocrity. Hide your character defects under matching underwear and expensive perfume. Do lots of sex with hardly any farts. Or body hair. Coquettishly demolish the bacon and eggs but be forever beach-body-ready like a cat about to pounce. You're aloof but attainable. Mysterious but knowable.

My own fridge is testament to my disposition. Never has an appliance typified my personality as well as the chrome sarcophagus humming in the corner of my kitchen. God only knows what I'd be without you, my igloo. Overexcitement at the John Lewis January sale saw my husband and me spaffing double our budget on an excessively large fridge, preparing for some imagined future where our entire family survives a nuclear holocaust by hiding in the salad crisper and living off the vast quantitates of food like an emergency escape pod. Luckily, the fridge has its own power cell and independent water subsystem. The elevator is fitted as standard, but the inflatable evacuation slide that doubles as a life raft cinched the deal. Please remove high heels before exiting the craft. Our fridge is slightly smaller than a Tesco Metro, but has more aisles and its own bakery, and it's replaced self-service with room service, with an efficient-but-discreet butler and a maid that doesn't complain to management when you crack on to her. The fridge is streamlined. The fridge is showy. The fridge is practical. The fridge is a self-portrait.

I want to give you a rundown of the gourmet-signalling and all the morsels of personality housed within our fridge. Please do not ask what I spend to achieve this foodie equilibrium: Ocado receipts, in silence, are quickly torn up. In the last month I've spent more than it costs to get Yeezy's, but less than Anna Nicole Smith inherited from her husband.

Very boring sex perfunctorily manoeuvres top-to-bottom, and I see no reason to break ranks for this chilled expedition through our fridge. Like newsagent porn, the fridge's top shelf is hot and cheesy: namely, mustard and fromage. Amongst the deliberately shambolic canopy of trophy sauces and condiments there are also whimsical Harry Potter jars containing vinegars of translucent yellows. On a clear day you can see through the liquids all the way to the back of the fridge. In these jars silhouetted pickled vegetables float straight to the top like nepotistic offspring. As part of a short-lived Martha Stewarting period I did a deep dive on DIY pickles, trapping spring's harvest in stock-piled Bonne Maman jars. Red onions were a cinch, and the pickled jalapenos still come out when I'm feeling Mexican, but dill pickles were the king: vinegary phalluses that fuck your mouth. Compared to raw cucumber, gherkins are twice as charming for being half as good for you. I love them more than teenage girls love belly tops. They are the greatest reward after a long day of reading you exes' horoscopes to see if they're still arseholes. Accidentally inhaling the vapours as pickling vinegar bubbled away on the hob was quite WWI mustard-gas attack, possibly stripping out all vital mucus and membrane from my lungs. I have culinary PTSD but I soldier on, expiration date unknown.

Centre-stage in the fridge is a thirty-pack of Diet Coke, which sounds like a lot. But it's my black petrol, keeping me bubbly since 1999. I always sip from tins so I don't feel completely addicted because I'm completely addicted. I only ever bought cigarettes in ten-packs when I was a smoker, because denial is more addictive than nicotine. Purchasing a full litre of black mischief would show the jitters in my caffeine-withdrawal hand. I went cold turkey on Diet Coke a few Januarys ago to prove to myself I could, but after a single sip in early Feb I shot back up to four a day. I've heard Diet Coke morphs your DNA, but I keep thinking, *What's my DNA ever done for me? Where was my DNA when I got mugged? Where was my DNA when I had my appendix out?* OK, I've never been mugged or had my appendix out, but we all know my DNA isn't to thank for that. I'll reconsider my position when I cough up a diamond of compressed Diet Coke syrup or birth a squid-baby, but some problems you can learn to live with, like air pollution or Jeremy Kyle.

My husband and I held a minute's silence when Carluccio's stopped doing tins of buffalo butter, dabbing at our eyes and ending our monthly pilgrimages to the deli in Angel, the 'affordable Hampstead' of London. After a suitable period of mourning we regrouped. Now we always have proper, proper cow's butter, preferably from a farm with a

— 66 —

name like Heavenshire Uttermilk, with those little salt crystals bursting like a Body Shop bath bead on the tongue. I like to think the dairy cows are happy and full to the brim with regurgitated organic grass while they get their teats wrung by virgin milkmaids. Each time my knife glides across my Borough Market sourdough toast I hear their bovine bliss, their mindful moos. One day I'm going to make sweet, passionate, sweaty, methodical love to the sound of those cows in that field. Emotions and butter churning at once.

One door shelf of the fridge has the paraphernalia for martinis – well, posh olives. I love a martini when I'm out, but only ever have them at home on Christmas Eve when I'm feeling particularly Gatsbyish. There are also plane-trolley-size cans of slimline tonic so you don't ever have to reopen a bottle of flat tonic and bastardise your Tanqueray. Again, this happens twice a year at most. This impression of icy classic cocktails at my fingertips is a direct descendant of the scene in *The Talented Mr Ripley* where Jude Law says he would fuck the icebox. I sometimes call the fridge the icebox like I live in fifties San Remo and get to sleep with Gwyneth Paltrow. Men, on the whole, are sick of being told Dickie Greenleaf and Steve McQueen are the pinnacles of style and masculinity. I think of myself as completely above these tired tropes, but it's this masc delusion that keeps me searching for Anderson & Sheppard pyjamas on eBay (very Greenleaf) and thinking I'll one day find white jeans that actually work for me (very McQueen). As an emerging gay the *Ripley* narrative spoke to me: all that Italian summer, cobbled piazzas, tuxedoed opera and latent homo-ness. That first bloom of desire becomes a Rosetta Stone of your sexuality, forever seared onto your gonads like cattle branding. In honour of the film I drank a lot of whisky soda in my twenties, and I adopted a pinky ring, but I never once touched the sax. Maybe years down the line I'll be murdered by my Stan in a boat and he'll assume my identity, the first act in an oddly relatable avalanche of evil deeds. Did you even go to Harvard, Tom?

Labels and packaging are important for fridge navigation too – Robinson's has the racist cartoon but Tiptree is a hoot. Jam is a gift from God, and can glow up a carb like tinsel on a picture frame. Jam allows fruit to outlive normal human life expectancy like Isabella Rossellini in *Death Becomes Her*. *Sempre viva! Live forever!* Sugar-wise the king of all packaging is the bees feeding off the lion's carcass on Lyle's Golden Syrup – Out of the Strong Came Forth Sweetness – but that's all the way over in the larder, which is a primary school's harvest festival assembly divided into tins. The broad beans are sleeping in a blankety bed. Well, not a bed. The larder is a vintage school cupboard I purchased on eBay for a sum of money that would make Meghan Markle blush. Save me from myself. Rather than simple, biblical-era ingredients for meals based on the fasting experiences of the Old Testament, the larder's packed with a million types of convenience food. Dried fruit and nuts, bars of dried fruit and nuts that look like they've been chewed already and spat into a bar shape. Coconut 'sugar', cashew 'milk', cauliflower 'rice'. Look at this trove, treasures untold, how many almost identical bags of pasta can one cupboard hold? And fourteen types of olive oil are a necessity, because failing to prepare is preparing to fail.

For lovers of the planet, fruit in plastic is incredibly triggering, an absolute no-no. Masses of my food deliveries arrive in food condoms, our fridge a mere pit stop en route to the floating island of plastic. Excessive packaging leads to global warming, climate change and, ultimately, an extinction-level event. Here we are now, acid rain us. The alarm sounds and I hustle my sleepy kids into the salad crisper where we remain till the planet rebirths months later. We'll emerge unscathed and inherit the earth, our DNA forever warped, our scars largely psychological. We'll repopulate the planet with our squid-like Diet Coke offspring, a world reborn from Adam and Steve, the only lovers left alive. To avoid the end of the planet, I tend to sneak excess packaging out under the recycling, like Lindsay Lohan attempting to abduct those Syrian children off the streets of Paris. We're zero plastic, naturally. And zero waste. A paper bag, not a paper plate. Actually, no bag. No plate. Just carry your yoghurt home in your hands. Think like a fairytale peasant before anything magical happens to them. Jack carried the beans in his pocket. Cinderella ate soot. Simplicity is key.

The freezer is a microcosm of my neuroses, an unflinching portrait of who I want to be, and a distraction from the inescapable passing of time. Literally everything is frozen, unageing in a perpetual electric winter. Each inhabitant is locked at full ripeness like the smiling woman in a thumbed photograph in a WWII soldier's pocket. The freezer is a well-stocked arsenal of ammunition for gorgeous impromptu meals with unexpected guests. A shoal of pink prawns and avocado halves I'll whip into a shrimp cocktail because cocktails you eat are chic as hell. We have fish fingers that we use to make fish tacos because tacos, corn-full moons of happiness, bring out the best in humanity. Who among us has never shotgunned a taco? Ice cream is a mouth-gift. As are frozen cherries. Gold, frankincense and brrrrrrr. There are also frozen pools of low-calorie, low-carb, low-fun soups for the days I choose hungry over happy. We eat pint after pint of dal now, which I batch-cook in a great Le Creuset vat, pretending to be a chef, tasting the lumpy slop and doing a chef's kiss. I have the sexy voluptuousness of Nigella Lawson spliced with the militant army sergeant Gordon Ramsay. I'm essentially a coy prick. Two-person portions of dal line the back wall of the freezer like sandbags in a flood, but they protect us from junk food when we're hungover. Devouring dal makes you feel like a just-back-from-spiritual-enlightenment nonconformist in a Joni Mitchell mould. Like living on Hydra wearing white linen and no shoes and smoking a shisha with the other global strays while Joni tinkles on the piano. Dal is served and you laugh and toast to nothing and smash your empty glasses down.

Much like the Little Mermaid I'm pescatarian (there's no red meat under the sea). I do crave meat, and I occasionally dream I'm in the rose-petal bed from *American Beauty* but it's slices of pepperoni, not flowers. But the last time I had a steak I got stomach cramps and was awake all night trapped inside my head with feelings of remorse. I love making new veg-aquarium friends, bonding over our teensy-tiny carbon footprints, swapping barbecued monkfish recipes and some-times just texting each other *god I love mammals*. We're all agreed Clarice could've prevented the silencing of the lambs had she chosen a pescatarian path. My freezer is nicknamed The Meg on account of the vast quantities of seafood. Peak mollusc. The depths are an Escher of Linda McCartneys, though the veggie sausages won't be one of the delicate little *amuse bouches* I'll rustle up for impromptu guests, as phallic foodstuffs can be a distraction.

Ironically, because of the social broadcasting of our ongo-ing renovation – the doorless bathroom that overlooks the bedroom and hall, fissures in the ceiling that expose the rafters – we haven't actually had any impromptu guests. My neighbour came to the door and couldn't hide her astonish-ment when she caught sight of the barren staircase behind me. I was trying to block her entrance, a bouncer saying she looked too drunk to get in, sweetheart, but that didn't work. I tried to distract her with an icy shard of frozen dal, but it was too late. Now she knows we're screwed house-wise, the keeping up of appearances has failed. She swung by a few weeks later and tried to give me her old blinds, for God's sake. The shame of it. Anyway, the ancient bohemian ideal of casual socialising went out the window with the invention of mobile phones. We always have warning shots (texts) fired before guests descend, leaving ample time to Mufasa the mess so that everything the light touches looks presentable.

The closing act of the fridge is the two boxes of St John wine, permanent tenants that typify my aspirations to be unflashy and traditional, exactly like a rosé in a cardboard box. A chilled magnum of champagne is a dick move, same with too many bottles of this wine we can't pronounce. Too ostentatious, like the French aristocrats who got beheaded or Marie Antoinette's cake. Like a good selfie, the best results turn the flash off. Less is more. A box of wine is deliberately gruff but also quietly decadent, expelling small quantities at your leisure because true adulthood is moderation. It's not modesty or minimalism, it's just a reduction of faff. And that's the goal of refinement. Less extraneous moving parts. Less bells. Less whistles. More usefulness and longevity. The new display of wealth is stealth.

People Taking Pictures of People Taking Pictures of the *Mona Lisa*

Every time Venice floods, people still wade through the perineum-deep water to get to Louis Vuitton. All those sopping tourists with boxes turbanned on their heads, paddle back to their chocolate-box palazzos and their iPhones. Floodwater can't get between me and my monogrammed weekender, nonchalantly slung over the back of a chair. The 2018 false missile alert in Hawaii saw Pornhub searches go through the roof, people literally searching lesbians smashing as they wanked themselves towards imminent death. Your knuckles, not your life, flashing before your eyes as you die.

When something dramatic happens we reach for our phones, but not to dial 999. We're compulsively reporting to our followers. We're as addicted to posting our own news as to checking each other's. These days you can't sit through a film at the cinema without seeing someone's face lit like a personal Diwali, though the feed we're returning to like a toxic ex isn't particularly illuminating. Culture is flatlining, its pulse limping to a halt like *ER* without George Clooney.

Somebody (I think it was Channel 4) decided equality was the goal, that our boundaries should come down and the divisions between us be dissolved. We all nodded because what else do you do? It all made an ebbing politically correct sense. But the great levelling that followed is making everything bland, flavourless, like being waist-deep in vanilla custard. Flatline culture is the result of all things being equal, like Animal Farm just after the revolution, because the mechanic of our feed erodes all barriers between all content great and small. The important things and the frivolous trifles bleed together like doctors without borders. Our newsfeed is a stag do where you were drinking vodka on the coach at 11 a.m. and calling each other mate, but at 2 a.m. in the club the magic has gone, everybody's out of energy, but no one can retreat. You shuffle about without any good moves. The feed's lost its kick, too. It doesn't floss or pirouette. Like the bleak back end of a house party, there are no peaks and troughs, just events that nobody should bother to record. A conga line of complacency.

Our infinite access to culture has become a duneless Saharan plain. A long and winding road with no forks. Ten thousand spoons when all you need is a knife. When you're online tidal waves have the same dimensions as a crème brûlée. The forest-fired Amazon is equal to a half-eaten prawn toast in Chinatown. The woman in San Francisco whose layered sandwiches I keep screengrabbing jostles with the Myra Hindley painting using kids' handprints. We glide forward, thumbing past passively equilateral squares on a conveyor belt. Hierarchy dissolves in this environment of endless posts like a Narnian winter with no Christmas. There's no difference in the way we're presented with totems of culture, so their meaning settles like a flat concrete floor. Drop a marble and it rolls nowhere. *There's breaking news, Brexit, Beyoncé. Netflix, Nutella, nuclear threat. Rice cakes, birthday cakes, babycakes.* Posts are a swarming mass of indistinguishable birds on *Springwatch*. The floating island of plastic is in bed with the cat from *Sabrina*. Ross's leather pants and Trump's Sellotaped tie raise eyebrows to the same height. Pamela Anderson runs in slow motion while people reveal their #MeToo experiences. There's no flightpath or final destination. Just another departure lounge, another layover, a perpetual take-off.

In our overfed dystopia we no longer hunt or gather for survival. We collect only in order to feed our own feeds. We're not only recording the big life events or revealing the gender of our offspring with coloured smog in a balloon – we're just as thrilled to announce the mulch. We will share anything: pictures of ourselves, our shoes, our curated homes. A sexy witch costume at Halloween. A steaming dim sum. A slightly damp Louis Vuitton scarf from Venice. We partake in a ceremonial self-disembowelling of everything we got for our birthdays, or read on holiday, or gobbled at lunch. We DM breaking new(d)s. And when all else fails, we fill the feed with videos of other people filling the feed. People taking pictures of people taking pictures of the *Mona Lisa*. Someone doing a selfie outside Auschwitz.

The boyfriends of Instagram. It's no longer showy or gaudy to reference yourself, to see something beautiful or noteworthy and immediately devise a strategy to inject yourself into proceedings – a selfie, usually, but a witticism or a snippy aside works too. A pun is a dextrous tool. I can't remember the last book I read and didn't make a big thing of. Or the last pithy one-liner I concocted but didn't tweet. The last time I ate in a restaurant and didn't Instagram was never. To save time making a table look appetising I've started just reposting someone who's eaten there before, which is both efficient and apocalyptic. But whatever we do, personal broadcasting is the default result. This is not virtue-signalling, where you loudly exhibit your care for the planet and its inhabitants, nor is it as simple as punter-signalling, where you showcase your gains. Punter-signalling keeps you shopping on Black Friday and Cyber Monday and camped outside John Lewis on Boxing Day, wrapped in a sleeping bag like a pig in a blanket.

On the surface it's a display of ownership – I shop therefore I 'gram. Humans have always diarised, but now the mechanism is more efficient. Neolithic times were better because we lived offline and the prize possession was a sharpened stick to spear a fish and a greasy bear pelt. Nobody got fomo. These days the value system has shifted from surviving to showcasing. Everything in our sightline is potential content that signals our cultural self – art exhibits, magazines, succulents, even our vitamins. We're grabby toddlers, reaching out for every passing object, but ownership is realised only when we convert these things to content. The therapy of retail remains, but the show 'n' tell of extraneous human paraphernalia denotes taste. It's not seen as flashy to post a Monet at MoMA, Kate Moss on the cover of *The Face*, or a bowl of cherries. These posts are all Jenga bricks in your tower of cultural capital.

During study break at sixth form I would mindlessly flick between the different MTVs, and I'm still doing that on my phone, which allows more channels from more broadcasters. It's a dramatised personal page-turner, a beach thriller that keeps us gripped. Unlike a good episode of *Murder, She Wrote*, nothing is resolved. Jessica Fletcher keeps cycling forward on deflated wheels as more cadaver casualties of the infinite scroll wash up on the shore.

Ironically the feed never nourishes us, we are never really *fed*. It's chicken nuggets – palatable and moreish but no real sustenance. Like a Diet Coke, everything tastes fine but each sip lacks vital nutrition. You're invisibly getting gout from overconsumption like Henry VIII, but like a Spice Girl friendship, the feed never ends. It's an infinite marathon, where the reward of a foil blanket is forever on the horizon, a finish line is never crossed. Rather than collapsing from exhaustion midway and getting airlifted to hospital, you just keep forwarding while your trainers fray and your feet wear away to nubs. The feed is designed for habitual ease, an effortless routine you barely register. You're flumed down a Rapunzel plait of content strands. Your thumb is the touch payment. The feed is forever exhaling like it's trying to blow out all the candles on a birthday cake in one go and keep going to next year's party. But at no point do you feel suffocated. There's no sudden realisation that it's got dark outside and you haven't put the big light on. It's a rolling golden hour where everyone looks sun-kissed and thin. Water laps right up to your ears but you never drown because there's buoyancy. At school, I got put in bottom-set GCSE Geography – a long story for another time – but there was a boy next to me who would look at my work and then copy it *without* capitalised letters or punctuation. The feed is the same. Nothing but non-threatening lower case and no commas. Not even the back-pat of a friendly em dash signalling a pause.

The world gets bigger, we can physically see more of it, but it's also less impactful, each cultural treasure diluted by its numerous neighbours. Posts have a limited shelf life too. White-hot sparklers one minute, incinerated the next, scattered like funeral ashes. You can't wrap posts in clingfilm. They don't keep in the fridge. Like trying to force a butter knife through scaffolding, attempts to cut through the racket are futile. For disciples of content something godlike can occasionally transcend to iconic status. The Father, the Son and the Holy Post. The flatlined feed is briefly defibrillated by a duchess closing a car door, but there's no spike longer than twenty-four hours. A million memes are spawned like frogspawn and then we all move on.

I know what you did last summer. And the summer before that. And the year you celebrated your GCSEs. The feed is Never Land, where I don't have to grow up, or old. There's the supple skin and glossy mane of my youth. I'm peeking out from under a golf visor at a drum'n'bass night in Brighton. That one time in Mexico City. And the party where I wore a neckbrace. On the feed I'm forever twenty-one, never maturing like a cigar or a fine wine. Catch me outside downing super-sweet Malibu and lemonade before calling my mum to pick me up from the park.

Within this blizzard of everything-all-the-time-ness, rich people have struggled. Most people can afford to post on Instagram, so it's not cash that has the highest value. It's a modern conundrum: what to post when you live in a gilded cage? I get the impression that despite the gout, Henry VIII didn't care about being cool or relevant, he just wanted to show off his jewels and Britain's dominance in a time before the potato was globalised. If technology had allowed, he would have livestreamed the beheadings on Instagram and there'd be an account of Catherine of Aragon revenge looks that we'd all rave over and forget in a week. These days the upper class has evolved, because being filthy rich with a charmed life isn't very rock 'n' roll. As a moneyed person, you no longer commission Holbein to spend three months painting a tableau of your wealthy lifestyle, you just grab an iPhone and downplay *everything*. The idea is to live like common people and do whatever common people do. Girl with a Claire's earring. It's this kind of reverse elitism that sees teenagers in yacht clubs wearing Supreme. Or Grimes couple up with Elon Musk. Success signalling isn't cool. Being flashy is trashy. There's now a series of Hansel and Gretel breadcrumbs, strategically dropped, that quietly signal your status – charcoal toothpaste, a Dyson, almond butter. The desire for scarcity and rarity is ever-present, but it's interwoven with 'normal' stuff that's effortlessly imbued with meaning (De Cecco pasta, the odd Conran plate, personalised vitamins). Being truly cultured is the dominant narrative, cutting though the thoughtless din of the feed with accurate expressions of good taste.

A big foam finger towards wealth is athleisure wear, simply because it signals a life with relaxation at its core. Annoyingly, as a young(ish) black man I get followed round the supermarket by security if I'm in a hoodie, but for the wealthy, dressing down signals to others that you're an atom with a wellness nucleus. You don't need to wear proper clothes in the morning, because your afternoon is spent reclining for an ice facial. All of your daily pursuits are laid-back and minimal, so why bother getting changed? Wellbeing is the paramount endeavour when you don't spend all your time worrying about the gas bill. Having the time to focus on yourself is the ultimate prize in the lottery of life. The achievement of balance is the final boss of success. The holy trinity of a life of accomplishment is style, taste and culture, interdependent in a pyramid of quiet luxury. And don't be fooled, you need cash for all of these. It's imperative to post clues to your success on the feed. Your cultural capitalism is worthless without broadcast.

You're competing with Venetian floods and masturbatory nuclear oblivion. Light my phone up like Diwali. Bring on the puns.

The Ghost of Christmas Past

Like a best man's speech after three champagnes, winter tends to bang on a bit and overstay its welcome. But before you hit the bleak mid-section the early days are throbbing with icy romance. Your hay fever dissipates, replaced by a romantically hacking Brontë cough, a chesty call to honourable menfolk in spats as you stumble about the misty moors. Everything's gallant and heroic like Heathcliff and Cathy, or quietly homely like the house-swapped Cameron Diaz and Kate Winslet. Winter means thick curtains and thicker knits, big stupid scarves that drag in the gutter, and the whiff of Lemsip on your breath. Like the liquid core of a Strepsil, inside all of us is a self-caring basic bitch begging to be cradled by a pumpkin-spiced pyjama set. Heat tech is goals – side note: my mum asked me what heat tech is and I could only answer 'Heat technology' – and people can't stop talking about winter boots and shearling. A hip-flask of whisky toddy is one of your five-a-day, hugging you from the inside, slowly pickling your vital organs and preserving them like jam for spring.

December is the bell-end of the year, a time when social anxiety peaks and rationale goes out the window. Christmas is the pinnacle of early winter, but the booze Olympiad can be trying. The entire season is an Alcoholics Anonymous application process thinly veiled by religious iconography and Morecambe and Wise reruns. December's a four-week gallop, when you *have* to see every acquaintance you've ever met in your entire life like a hideous yuletide *Challenge Anneka*, the goal being to make it to the 25th without liver failure. For the duration of the aggressive social calendar, we're all trying to be Sarah Jessica Parker in *I Don't Know How She Does It*, balancing wholesome family life with political hot takes, and a killer body under the right cocktail trousers. It's a party flume of work people, old school friends, your kids' friends' parents, that uncle that never married, that aunt with the limp. Nobody is spared. A groundhog month of low-key soirées 'thrown together' by kitchen goddesses in their side-returns. Their homes stink of downplayed cash. Decor is that of a cosy snowed-in chalet somewhere in the Alps. Absence makes the heart grow fondue.

The oddest tradition of Christmas season has to be feeding people tiny portions of aromatically problematic food – the fish, the eggs, the fish eggs – and immediately standing them under mistletoe to snog. I just ate a miniature crab tostada – who wants to massage my tongue with theirs under this low-hanging plant? Mistletoe is the bane of the season: gnarly Chinese knotweed masquerading as a jolly winter rose. Standing under mistletoe next to a stranger is more awkward than splitting the bill with your parents at a non-birthday dinner. Honestly, who wants to kiss someone because of foliage? Mistletoe is a scumbag, a maggot, a cheap lousy houseplant. An unwanted Davina-McCall-on-*Streetmate* spectre haunting couples and singles alike, a boa constrictor crushing people together lip-to-cheek. Anyone who's had a common cold knows this is bad.

The absolute best thing about winter is that turtleneck season is also pretty-face season – all the hot summer bodies get wrapped up and there's nothing your scorching-hot peers can do about it. Winter is the great leveller, where everything pivots on the attractiveness of your face. Here they come, the beautiful ones. So not only do you have to lock eyes with every person in your life, you have to look like a million bucks too. And by the second week of December we exceed our recommended daily allowance of mingling. Despite quite a hefty resistance I exceed my allowance of eggnog too. Your allowance of sequins quadruples at this time of year, but people still manage to overdose, needing a shot of minimalism straight to the heart like Uma Thurman in *Pulp Fiction*. I love that attendees refuse point-blank to wear matte clothes. Matte is banished like Romeo from Verona after killing Tybalt. Anything below a semi-gloss is taboo. And like mince pies, the best Christmas outfits look like they've been liberally sprinkled with icing sugar. You need a stealth approach to survive the party season – think Sylvester Stallone in *Rocky* or Goldie Hawn in *Private Benjamin*. Cut to a training montage of you spaffing glitter, crushing velvet and sandblasting your face with Touche Éclat. Wrap your tired body like a present in John Lewis paper, preferably iridescent, and remember it's OK to do flats if you look rich. Rich-signalling comes from years of deeply developed taste, built up like layers of Farrow & Ball paint. You don't just pop the flats on, you live an informed and tasteful life and the flats are just a portal enabling mortals to glimpse your utter refinement.

People get quite het up about their faces ageing, but if you really want to stop time, do small talk at a party while you're still sober. Time grinds to a halt like Bernard's Watch. Small talk is an unnecessary evil, as devilled as the eggs displayed on a quietly antique tray. A purgatory of stilted questions and answers. It's not quite hell on earth, but the fiery flames of the underworld reach up to lick your throat and scorch your dry mouth while you grapple for socially lubricating vocabulary. Outside of what-do-you-do-oh-interesting and that's-a-very-nice-sparkly-dress there's little left to say. I sometimes resort to listing all the other Christmas parties I have to attend or have attended. Every stunted question feels like a prayer for your soul to ascend to heaven, far away from this closed-question limbo. Social purgatory. Most horror films have gore and teenage babysitters in their grundies, but true horror is small talk at a Christmas party. Trying to maintain an air of interest while desperately trying to catch the eye of your partner, or even a child you can pretend looks distressed so you can fake a rescue and reunite them with their parents.

Like hieroglyphics, small talk is a lost art. Trying to find common ground with a virtual stranger is hard, especially if they like fantasy role play or historical re-enactment. Most of the things I genuinely like are secret guilty pleasures and not suitable for party conversation – gossiping about frenemies, Ritter Sport Cornflakes, *The Good Wife*, anal. On that note, Christmas parties are like anal: once you get past the initial hurdle they're quite fun. If you're not feeling very jolly you act very jolly, and jolliness lifts you up like a pig in a blanket, seeping into your tired bones like chemo. Baileys is rocket fuel. Before you know it you're dancing like Fed Astaire to Paul McCartney and declaring you want your own album to be fifteen different versions of 'Candle in the Wind'. Followed by an EP of a cappella Christmas songs. On Christmas Day your family won't be able to hear the Queen's speech over the sound of your butt cheeks clapping while you twerk to 'Carol of the Bells'.

It's understandable that single Cinderellas, both male and female, tend to discreetly slip out of the ball for a Tinder hook-up. Winter is coming, but so are you, potentially. After chestnuts roast on an open fire, we retreat online and flirt on apps. Romance on the downlow with an indoor-faced app regular is preferable to being forcibly sandwiched to a random acquaintance for small talk. These relationships have a small cycle with a predictable formula. Hold me, thrill me, kiss me, kill me. The nitty-gritty of assisted masturbation comes at a price: every guy who offers to host also has the option to ghost. Isn't it wild how people who ghost you still watch every one of your Instagram stories? Like Keyser Söze these lovers disappear into thin air. Like that, he's gone. Despite this we keep trying to make Happn happen.

I always want to keep Christmas simple. I identify with the rejectionist Mormon back-to-basics approach that rejects modernity and its glitzy trappings. It's anti-Gatsby, zero jazz, anti-moths-to-the-flames-of-capitalism. Annoyingly, this essentials-only approach is what started nearly every suicide cult. It's humble in principle: you reject mainstream society and focus on a Flintstoneian self-sufficiency. You reap, you sow, you reap, you sow. But somewhere in the cycle a switch flicks and before you know it you're all downing cyanide to protest against an inhumane world and ascend to the celestial plain. Spiritual ascendance aside, a simple Christmas is what I need, and I have a habit of getting what I want.

Picture the scene: a rustic, humble home in a remote village that also has wifi and memory-foam mattresses. Christmas should always be musical (apart from the scum-bag faggot line in 'Fairytale of New York'), so an album of medieval flute serenades us while we prep the veg, laughing at our family in-jokes. Once dinner's in the oven I warm through the mince pies with the mincemeat I made from scratch on stir-it-up Sunday because I wasn't hungover. We listen to harpsicord, because harpsicord. Somebody artfully dishevels crackling on the turkey, arranging it like Buffalo Bill cutting a suit pattern. Somewhere upstairs a French horn sounds. We have cleverly mismatched presents under the tree, with all the best baubles above cat height. Choirs of angels sing in exaltation. Christmas morning is always about looking for a way to casually gram my latest expensive purchase. I receive my original signed Hockney. Sleigh bells ring, can you hear them? The whole day is a scene in a Christmas film where even the poor people look fabulous, little urchins and cherubs who can be pacified with a slice of turkey as we all ignore the austerity crisis for one afternoon. A cello is playing (I'm not sure how).

I don't want to paint myself out like Tiny Tim, but I did not grow up like this. I did not grow up rich. I did not grow up with a real tree or a turkey or trendy toys (I begged for light-up LA Gears). One year we had sausages and vegetables for Christmas lunch because we couldn't afford turkey. We never had Christmas traditions per se, so now I'm hung up on them in a way that sucks out all the joy. I recognise that it's hardly time to get the violins out, but my single-parent upbringing always draws into sharp focus at Christmas, as most family relationships are wont to do. We were many things, my mum and I, but we weren't rich, and I was all too aware of it. At six, my mum asked me what I wanted to be when I grew up and I said middle class.

Rich is a sliding scale of course, and no matter where you are on the ladder, there's always someone richer. Someone with a moat. Someone with a car. Someone with different rooms for cooking and eating and sleeping. Nowadays, when we all bundle into my mum and stepdad's house at

Christmas, the airbed in the spare room is still better than the corridor behind the sofa we called my room for six years growing up. I remember getting holes in my shoes and waiting for payday for new ones. I remember going maybe three months without a haircut. Not poor, not loaded. Getting by but not quite thriving. My mum and I were a tag team, and though she shouldered the responsibly, we shared the worry. I never wanted for attention – as you can probably guess. And I was never, ever a sad kid. Thoughtful and introverted and self-sufficient, yes, but not sad. No LA Gears, but I wasn't worn down by the situation. It didn't erode me. And things did change. My mum slogged her guts out. We met my stepdad and we were sponges for his traditions, keen to soak up familiar family customs. A roast every Sunday was breaking news for us. A glass of wine at night. Christmas at his house in the West Country. And again the next year, and the next. Always partial to a performance, we still talk about going to midnight mass every year, but we've never once talk about Jesus. Traditions are familiar things you can expect and plan for, rather than respond to. A life less reactionary. We had genuine ascension, my mum and I, and I've capitalised on every last drop of that privilege.

Whether or not I mention my early (crack-of-dawn) days in council housing or my house in France depends on the room. I dial up my roots or my current status based on mood. At times I want to be the interloper who's made it, at others I want to pass go and collect £200 without a fuss. I flip between wanting to join and wanting to sabotage.

My mum is more anarchic, but she also loves *foie gras*. My social standing (my class?) is a ball tossed into the air that has never come down. It never settles like snow. I'm still figuring the dualities out. The poorness alongside the frequent European mini-breaks. The baggy school uniform next to the yacht. (I love saying 'yacht' like it's not a floating seventies caravan). See how I downplayed it, even just now? That part of the constant balance of poorness and privilege. I love rolling my eyes at my own house hell, mid-renovation, knowing that the chance to graft and pick out architraves is a sign of my success too. To say I'm ambitious is misleading, because it suggests I know where I'm going. Ambition is a tool to get success, and actually it's the graft I get off on. The hard, hard work is the payoff. Graft is a big takeaway from my upbringing. Graft is a great way to smash the worry out of your life. The desire to work like a dog is in ingrained in me. I have proper guilt when I'm not working. I feel bad when I indulge myself, and yet I love to indulge myself. The crippling guilt of it all coming too easily. Do we really deserve the things we didn't absolutely slog our guts out for?

I don't think I'm a champagne socialist. And I got a genuine thrill when someone called me a yuppie recently, like I'd passed an invisible test. I can walk into a room and not stink of my past, hooray. But then I felt guilty. The past was great. When your previous family situation gets better the safety net it provides gets stronger and you can soar higher without fear. Is evolving out of my working-class roots the same as forgetting them? Am I deliberately shrugging off the past? Are my own trivial pursuits – the house, the home, the husband – built on a bedrock foundation of privilege that some people dream of, and others quietly pity?

This has something to do with the American Dream, a system within which you can outgrow your hometown and home life and ascend like an angel to the spiritual kingdom of a big city. Usually fame and fortune. Everybody wants this for you, and a certain shrugging-off of roots is expected. Andy in *The Devil Wears Prada*. Calamity Jane shrugging off the creek. Americans never apologise for success as it is based on graft and focus and your future, not your past. For the English, ascension is different. Our society is so focused on heritage and family that when people ascend they can only really get rich. Who your parents are doesn't change. There's a big difference between *getting* rich and *being* rich. As I mentioned, being rich is about a huge matrix of social codes. In London there are always dinners to attend, and parties to party, and culture to be snorted. But no matter how affluent you become, and whatever your social standing, you're still new money. There's a seat at the table but your breeding is lacking, or you went to the wrong school. You never have the family heritage that others have cultivated over centuries. Americans want to see a biracial actress marry Prince Harry. But she can't shake her brash family, and the whole of Britain is staring.

You can be the inescapable chatty extrovert at the champagne soirées, the saviour of small talk. But you'll never have that lineage: the zip wire between you and your roots stays taught and unchanging. Our culture is based on silent signals of class and heritage, and family history isn't something you can fake at this party or the next one. Despite your outward assimilation you're the poor relation (Tiny Tim again), but I'm not complaining. The intersection of the class Venn diagram is where the waves gently lap at the shoreline and you can earn nice holidays without the irksome shackles of a trust fund. And though I'd still like to meet Donna Tartt at a Christmas party and have such an earth-shattering spiritual connection over the mulled prosecco that she retires before midnight to rewrite *The Secret History* with me as a central character, I'm happy to leave the shindig as a guest who didn't come across as the firestarter of the class war. These nights end, as the often do, palatably enough, with the host begging you to please eat the last mince pie as you spill out onto the pristine Hampstead street and into your awaiting carriage.

The bit straight after Christmas is the best. The subtext of every outfit is gout, stilton forming between the toes. You lie dormant in the perineum between Christmas and New Year, your insides base-coated in chocolate coins. There's the old traditions of turkey curry and bubble and squeak and that existential cousin who refuses to participate in gifting, and the insufferable search for the perfect white jean for your equestrian legs in the January sales. But you never forget the Christmas you had sausages.

Being Tall

Objectively I'm the hottest of my friends, but they're all women, so the usual rivalry is cancelled out. Like most people, I want to be even hotter because hotness is a social currency more valuable than free drinks tickets or the euro. Hotness eases the assault course of modern life; the terrain is flatter for the hot as they saunter past the average faces on the monkey bars. I want to be the kind of hot where people post 'Wow, just wow' on my selfies. I want to be the guy who knowingly ignores your rapture when I take off my top at the beach. I'll chivalrously help you up when you trip over the rolling planes of my abs like a draught excluder. I want to be the kind of hot where you pretend you hate getting hit on all the time and you hate free Ubers and unsolicited dick pics. The kind of hot where you do a chopsticks walrus in a Vietnamese restaurant and still look fit because your raw hotness burns through the comedy bit. The hotness level where you're objectified in a woke way. Why be a tepid footbath when you can be the hot wax in a Ricky Martin video? I want the *faux*-trauma of being thought of as just a pretty face even though I read the *New Yorker*. I want people to drown like innocent witches in the depths of my eyes. I want to talk absolute shit while people just nod because they're transfixed by the simmering heat I give off like a good jambalaya. My ideal temperature is don't-have-to-work-but-choose-to Fahrenheit. I don't necessarily want a sugar daddy, but I'd like it as a fallback option. I'd take a manageable stalker, the kind who sends loads of letters that I secretly find flattering and stands outside being benign. I'd take those insidious Tumblr accounts where they jizz on celebrity faces in magazines. A blue plaque memorialising my creation would not go amiss at the hospital where I was born. Perhaps a little Hockney portrait in Tate Britain (a sketch, I'm not a diva), that would up admission numbers as coachloads of travellers pilgrimage towards my likeness, so that they may gaze upon my hotness. And a commemorative pound coin with my striking profile is a must. Why let the passing of time rob future generations of my beauty?

Like most things it's always better to look as if you haven't tried too hard, as if being hot is an accident, erotic ley lines converging on your being by chance. My personal regime is an own goal of self-trickery – hours of online research and purchasing expensive medicated creams that I then nonchalantly spritz on every night in front of my husband like it's no big deal. Incidentally I'm also addicted to hand cream, which might be my most bourgeois confession: I slather expensive scented lard up to the biceps like I'm preparing to birth a calf. I can pretty much convince myself I'm low-maintenance until I travel and half my hold luggage is Biologique Recherche and free Kiehl's testers. That's when the grim, dogged complexity of my moisturisation draws into sharp focus. When I die, give my eye cream to the poor and remember I was moist.

My friends are better at maintenance. Farmers nurturing the paddocks of their own faces. There was once a day-long (inconclusive) WhatsApp chat about retinol, but on the whole their regimes remain a mystery. It's weird how we call them beauty *secrets*, as if a healthy glow is as mysterious as Stonehenge, or unsplit ends the riddle of the Pyramids. White teeth are the Loch Ness monster. Beauty is deliberately cryptic. How we achieve the shape of our bums or the tautness of our faces remains hidden like the Enigma code: a mystery for outsiders to try to crack.

There's a secrecy to what's happening below the surface of a face. We're all assigned to the covert operation of preserving ourselves, undercover agents of our own hotness. Our beauty regimes and self-maintenance are part of an interior secret world, like the puppeteer inside Big Bird. Ostensibly living lives of lobster decadence and champagne hedonism while maintaining the toned body and bowel rhythm of a strapping farmhand. Diamond-hard partying with a teenager's skin and waist size. But late nights are the opposite of youth serum. We want a disproportionate correlation between cause and effect: big lives without them being written all over our faces. Personal restraint is key, we tell ourselves. Our bodies should be monuments to self-control.

We're freewheeling through each impulsive, spontaneous moment, but ultimately steering the ship with steely determination. It's a desire to remain restricted, like the embryo laboratory in *Jurassic Park*. Restraint is moderation, keeping us from gobbling great fistfuls of cake or shagging in the street or overdosing on heroin. A slice of cake, not a fistful, or perhaps no cake at all. You would be hotter if you went to the gym more. You would be hotter if you conditioned your hair. You would be hotter if you washed your face. Life itself would be better if only you could resist sugar. Or Netflix. Or the ease of an Amazon purchase. You just lack restraint.

I want to be the kind of hot where people ask, 'What's your secret?' When they do, I'll never say hardcore hot yoga, intermittent orthorexia and litres of Diet Coke. I'll never say skipped meals and cocaine, or the week I spent downing sachets of powdered appetite suppressant. I won't mention the constant irritability of double espresso on an empty stomach. I'll always say water. Perhaps a sip of apple-cider vinegar first thing, but mainly water. I say things like 'moisturiser can only do so much, you need to start from the inside'. Being a hydration ambassador makes me appear both spiritual and carefree. I'm imbued with a biblical understanding of myself. I'm attracted to the simplest of things and live a humble, uncomplicated life as a result. It's like I'm made up of foraged grains and unpasteurised spring water rather than mercury-laced sushi rolls and battery-hen eggs. Conscious simplicity is the life goal, achieved through troglodyte gastronomy.

Water is magic. An incantation for vitality. Instant vigour, with Jesus baptising your insides. When you drink water your pot belly recedes and your hairline grows back like the tide rolling in on a late-summer Cornwall beach. The calluses strip themselves from your feet and your kidney stones, those pesky hard rocks, turn into gems. With each sip the whites of your eyes get whiter and people say you look younger. Obviously your penis gets bigger, or your boobs go up a cup size (the rising oestrogen level in London's water table is a helping hand here). With water you are seven feet tall and newly ambidextrous. You know French and Italian, and conversational Russian. You finally quit cigarettes and toxic lovers. You stick to New Year's resolutions. Pure goodness reinvigorates your carcass like a shot of vodka and half a pinger at Fabric (without the inevitable please-Jesus-let-me-die comedown). You feel like you're doing hot vinyasa flow in a skimpy leopard-skin leotard while listening to 'Upgrade U' on repeat. A muscular mortal coil ready to spring into action.

Full disclosure: water is not the only weapon in the beauty arsenal. Natural biology plays a big part. My natural body shape is carnival mirror, with super-long legs and a super-long torso. Beauty trends come and go, but the power of being tall is a timeless classic, like *Gone with the Wind* or florals for spring. Being tall is great because you never need to get near the front at public events. If anything, you stay near the back and turn around doing *sorry eyes* to anyone caught behind you staring at the muscles in your knee-pit. You can be a complacent party-goer but people instantly gravitate towards you and your staggering inseam despite your weird laugh and blatant offish-ness. The tall reek of fun, and you can see our beaming faces over the tops of the normal people's heads, anchored by our giant tall-person feet in Ronald McDonald shoes. When you're tall it's not the weather that's different up here, it's the climate. Above average height scientifically makes your whole life better: tall people are higher earners and are more confident after years of preferential treatment. And all tall people have a leggy heritage: Jerry Hall could be their mum, or a close aunt, or a family friend, or maybe walked past the hospital where they were born. Rumours swirl that King Triton is their dad, because if he had legs not a tail he'd exceed seven foot. Tall people lank their way through life, collecting the knobbly-kneed royalties due to their stature, legs eleven out of ten. We are default chivalrous, and capes become us in a dramatic-and-dashing *Sleepy Hollow* way. We're default gregarious, which is actually a tragic by-product of altitude sickness. We're default hot because God stretched us for greatness on the medieval rack of evolution. Being tall is like wearing killer heels *all the time*, but never getting tired like the shoeless women outside kebab shops in broken-Britain tabloid exposés. (Those women always look quite hardy, to be fair, but that doesn't make a great headline.) Being tall is like the streets are paved for you with the Yellow Pages, you're on the yellow brick road and everybody else is a Munchkin.

It's like you've doubled up on those stacked orthopaedic shoes like toxic men next to tall women. You are two Tom Cruises, or both Olsen twins under a Burberry trench. Every additional inch up the body is a floor of virtuousness, tiers of pure integrity all the way to the nosebleeding altitude of the penthouse, with its telecommunication mast signalling brilliance. When you walk into a room people implicitly warm to you, so you don't have to prove your worth with a well-placed anecdote that's the perfect triptych of alluring, self-deprecating and non-threatening.

Being tall is like being average height but way better. Every interaction in your life is rose-pink Technicolor. When you're tall there's a latent suggestion your coping skills are exemplary, as are your kisses. The key skill of the tall is to graciously shrug off desperately transparent compliments from strangers. Being average height is not an option because it diverts attention to taller places. Being average is just an eroded version of greatness, pitiful teeth of leftover cliff poking up out the sea. Nobody buys an average hits album. I wonder why, he's the average dancer. Someone invented a saying about small packages to placate tiny people. One assumes it was conjured up by a group of near-midgets barely peeking over the table at a pub, tiptoeing to clink glasses. In the nineties we had Small Man Syndrome, based on the idea that short men are angry and will eventually get het up when they're out on the town. Nowadays, thanks to the Obamas, we all pretend short people have equal rights.

Despite the perks of being a tallflower, there are drawbacks. I don't enjoy being folded in half on the rush-hour tube with my chin against my shin. Nor do I love the exposed beams of a country cottage. I once got hit in the head by a lorry's side-view mirror as it passed. That was embarrassing. It's actually very hard to be tall and cute. Ever seen a tall, cute baby? Or a cute pair of size-11 shoes? I rest my case. The Christmas after I turned sixteen, I temped at the Disney Store and had to wear a cardigan and Mickey Mouse ears for three months. There was a tall employee we all called Steps and we made him get things down for us from the top shelves in the stockroom. Those were less woke times, when the Spice Girls were all solo and people said things like *fuck-me boots* and *disco minge*. All the men wanted to be Mike Skinner. All the women did too. The nickname Steps wouldn't fly in today's politically-correct culture. Diane Abbott would get a nosebleed. Jameela Jamil would tweet. I'd get sued and Disney would fire me and publicly apologise and donate cash to a people-of-reduced-height charity.

I only temped at Disney in the dying embers of the nineties, and though I was tall for my age, outside of work my life wasn't full to the brim with excitement. All I did was stay up until 10 p.m. to masturbate to *Eurotrash*. We all thought planes were going to crash out of the sky at midnight on New Year's because of the millennium bug, but I was a cool adolescent so I pretended not to care. On actual New Year's Eve my parents gave me a bottle of champagne to share with my friends and we traipsed about the town doing three-swig-pass and very little else. At midnight we ended up in a big crowd near a bus stop. Despite being tall I could hear fireworks but I didn't see any. Not a single plane fell from the sky in an exciting fireball. It was a bit shit to be honest, but that's sixteen for you.

So being a tall person isn't all top-shelf perks. I keep fantasising about someone picking me up like a baby, like in *Gulliver's Travels* when Gulliver goes to Brobdingnag. It's not a sex thing, like those baby-men on Channel 5, it's just something I think I need as the evenings get darker and the nights get colder. I would also give it all up for slightly smaller thighs. Is that normal? My yoga pilgrimages make me feel amazing, but my thighs are more drumsticky than is desired. They're unusually beefy for a pescatarian. I look at them, willing transformation like Magic Eye. Smaller thighs are at the top of my to-do list, but I can't be arsed to make any real sacrifices. I've researched *less muscular thighs*, and essentially you have to exhaust your legs like a marathon runner with relentless low-impact exercise. No squats. No swimming. Absolutely no cycling uphill. I tried it for four days and I felt like Colin in *The Secret Garden*, all tired limbs and bad attitude. My legs looked the exact same. Was it worth it? No, but that has more to do with my lack of restraint – a couple of times I cheated and gobbled Babybels while cycling uphill. And four days isn't enough of a controlled experiment. Like a toddler, my mood is dictated by my meals. Fatigued means too many carbs, grumpy means not enough. Neither bodes well for smaller thighs. Should my quest for aesthetics outweigh any emotional baggage? Absolutely yes. Will I always fail? Yes. Will I keep pursuing better thighs? Abso-fucking-lutely. Is it boring to hear a gay whinge about being tall and having big thighs? It's too late.

Two Drinks-Drunk

Last summer I drank so heavily at a wedding in Spain I attempted the magician's trick of whipping the tablecloth out from under everybody's glasses. It was unsurprisingly misadventurous, resulting in a completely collapsed table, much spilled Prosecco and many a drenched Ganni dress. Thankfully, two other guests formed an impromptu first-responder team, surveying the wreckage and airlifting the smithereens of glass away in a makeshift bindle from a table-cloth like the stork bringing a baby.

Atonement for this particular party transgression came in the form of blanket denial, in the vein of Shaggy, but I knew I'd crossed a line. Not rock bottom, not even close. I've never drunk at a level where I needed to talk about it anonymously. In theory I'd go to AA for the undivided attention, everyone manoeuvred into a listening circle while I, an AA soloist, regale the group with tales of failed magic tricks at weddings. Are AA meetings just sober people get-togethers where they collude in saying being sober is great, regardless of how great it actually is? The Freemasons, but they want everyone to stop drinking, so their secret handshake is a slimline tonic and a dash of bitters? Is bitters mildly alcoholic? Perhaps stick to bottled water from the Pacific island of Fiji. Abstinence is a form of self-flagellation, and I completely understand why people get off on it. I suspect sobering up is drier than the Sancerre you're banned from drinking, more like a crispy flannel on the side of the bath that keeps its shape when you pick it up. I'm a drinker who wants a wet January. An aquatic aeon. A Niagara night. We're not really meant to admit this. It's something to grow out of after university, like baggy jeans or Pot Noodle. Full-time crust-flannel sobriety isn't one of my aspirations. All the evenness of emotion that comes from unheavily drinking wouldn't suit me.

Sometimes I'm so hungover I can't stop my mind flashing to Gwyneth Paltrow's seizure in *Contagion*, so I can see the appeal of waking up Snow White-lucid and being so darn cute that the forest animals help me with the housework while I whistle. I would also love the optimised liver function, clearheadedness and wherewithal to make dauphinoise from scratch in an afternoon. I Google detoxes. I could handle a week of rejuvenation in Austria or an Austria-adjacent country where the landscape's piney and the air is bracing. I'd stay at a clinic where they take your blood and mix it with placenta, tailoring tonics to your genetic make-up administered intravenously while you spreadeagle in a white dressing gown. I'd be off the grog doing new-fangled autogenic therapies that sound like the names of celebrity kids. A week of fortifying massage, but the happy ending is a flight back to London and a martini at Dukes.

My party trick is stamina, but there's a reciprocal relationship between how long I've been drinking and how much of the real me is actually left. The problem with drinking is that it dulls you. Remember the urban legend of the GCSE student who stuck pencils up his nose in the exam and smashed them into his brain? I'm that sharp in the mornings and most of the day, but at twilight my edges are blunt as caveman flint. Around midnight I become an echo of my personality, a nicely dressed stealth-dancer, a streak of luxe fabric with a pearl earring. I say yes to tequila. I say yes to alcopops. I never miss a beat. The best me, the optimum party-self, the guy who's still listening to you, is a few drinks back. Pre-tequila. Back near the toasts, at the point when it was me speaking, not the booze. Rewind the night to dusk and catch me at two drinks.

It's not just weddings where it's great to be two-drinks drunk. Funerals are improved by a tipple. Bar mitzvahs, birthdays and baptisms are eased by a double buzz of beers. If someone is throwing a divorce party it doesn't matter what you drink because it will be a blow-dry and some stage-managed I'm-not-bitter bitterness. Passive aggression of the highest order. Two drinks is the drunk you need for social occasions. Two drinks flow and so does the conversation. You feel truly magical, rather than parroting magic tricks. Two drinks is a tier where you are charmingly louche and interested in other people, but not thinking about how much alcohol you've had or whether your last question was any good. Optimum inebriated. Premium pissed. Not too sober and not too drunk. Goldilocks's porridge but it's a toddy. The tipsy where you're light on your loafers but steady on your feet. Your pupils are dilated, but not your arsehole.

This is my personality at its best, often appearing at early-evening get-togethers or children's birthdays, as the under-fives double-drop Fruit Pastilles. Occasionally making an appearance before midday on vacation. I'm not debilitatingly self-conscious when I'm sober, but after two drinks I'm excellent. I'm me after finding a tenner on the street and immediately taking myself out for cheesecake. I'm me after a vigorous nit shampoo and three episodes of *The Crown*. When I was a smoker, smoking in bed was my most happy and disgusting pastime. I miss it dearly, but two drinks is a step in the right direction. A nirvana of self-ease. When I'm stone-cold sober I'm a pianist approaching the piano to play Chopin at the Albert Hall for the first time. Maybe his usual preparation rituals were slightly off – the steak he ate was too rare, the water he gargled too salty. Little moments of offness that tally up at the back of his mind. Out in the audience is his emotionally distant father, who's flown in from the Bajan yacht he shares with his new wife. Playing Chopin tonight is a big deal, but the pianist's fingers are shaking. The pressure has mounted. He needs two drinks because two drinks will transform him. His will fingers reignite and he'll play Chopin with a clarity that makes people throw roses on the stage and his father weep.

After two drinks the elusive 'best self' I search for in therapy is massaged into existence and is ready to grant three wishes to fellow two-drinkers. My nervous system isn't nervous. I'm funny but not in a competitive way. I'm loud but I can't drown you out. My inhibitions dip, but not to the point where I take my top off. I'm confessional but not at a Catholic level. People don't like to say it, but drinking is magic. Your state shifts from solid to liquid. Comatose to silver-tongued. Sensual but not slutty. The buoyancy of the post-coital on Christmas Eve. The *je ne sais quoi* of an ice-cold drink is transcendent and enhances your character. There's no smoke, no mirrors. Just you being your best, not held back by the sobering truths of your undrunk self. You're sparkling like champagne. You're scissors gliding across wrapping paper. Your collar slowly unbuttons itself. Your skirt gets an inch shorter. You have the balls to punch above your weight. You're a symphony. The rules of drinking are the same as the rules for vacations and jobs and general living: stay hydrated, don't be a dick.

Early doors is full of anticipation. It's a magnificent margin of time, like Britain between the two wars in the golden age of crime fiction. The two-drink window has the promise of a night that rolls out ahead of you in the mist. You're leaving a sherry out for Santa but you don't know what happens when you turn your back. There's a level of unpredictability that you don't get soberly checking your iCal before bed. You could end up at dinner with some YBAs talking about podcasts and Brexit before dancing all night and necking someone with bigger arms than your ex, waking up miles from home in a fur coat next to someone with the face of Brad Pitt and the temperament of Burt from Mary Poppins.

The pure charisma of two drinks is transient. But the scale always tips. Everyone thinks they're a great drunk and nobody *is* a great drunk. We never heed the trumpet of moderation – where's the fun in that? I passed the exam with moderate colours. I had moderate Christmas Eve sex. Thank you for my moderate orgasm. Sips turn into gulps. Gulps to glugs. Glugs turn into shots and the wheels come off. You lose your footing. Eat, drink and be lairy. Sometimes you need to escape yourself and enter a headspace that isn't about how you feel or your anxieties or building lasting relationships stirred through with meaning like raspberry ripple. You need the annihilating inebriation where it's impossible to be prickly, like a dethorned rose at the florist. At first you're Toni Collette and Rachel Griffiths maniacally lip-syncing to 'Waterloo' in *Muriel's Wedding*. Then you're Rizzo in *Grease*, singing to herself about staying out every night and taking cold showers. But you become a night terror, as gin pickles your internal organs. You suddenly have no gag reflex and a flexible spine, but you start talking about your exes. You invade a bouncer's personal space. You're blotto. You want to rally those around you. You want to form the kind of cross-socioeconomic, cross-cultural conga line that would make the UN blush. Instead you give a long but fact-free speech about institutional anti-Semitism in the Labour Party. It makes people wince. You give an even longer speech about AirPods and a shorter speech about those little hotel fridges you have to open with a key. You claim velociraptors would do a better job than the current Tory government. You Uber to Soho. You're legless like Lieutenant Dan. You ask why the floor is tilting. You Uber south of the river. Where are your shoes? You Uber down Sunset Strip like Hugh Grant. Why is a stranger holding your hair while you vomit? You Dementor through clubs like the undead in the Michael Jackson 'Thriller' video. You poke your ex on Facebook. You order a round of drinks for a group of people half your age on your work credit card. After a scrap in the loo over a lollipop you have to retire from public life like Prince Andrew. Hours later you wake up and it's already dark. You retrace your night via social media and start the apology-texting as you sip Purdy's.

A surefire way to avoid a hangover is gobbling from the snack-troughs that the waiters circle you with. Tiny Borrower food: cocktail sausages, mini burgers, itsy bitsy teeny weeny quiches. Your body is sacred – if not a temple then a generously sized multi-faith prayer room at an airport – and mini quiches are communion for drinking. By the time you realise you need a pint of water and a shrunken roast dinner served in a Lilliput Yorkshire pudding it can be too late. Maybe I've woken up a few times after a small night out that escalated, feeling less than resplendent. Not the bear with a sore head exactly, more the bear with last night's kebab matted into his fur, and a palpable sense of dread about being a dick to his other bear friends. Crusted crystals of sambuca creaking like an arthritic knee in the pit of my stomach. A cannonball of anxiety around my heart. A Trojan horse of dread wheeled in behind my temples. I often do yoga stretches before bed, and I've been known to wake up mid-morning in child's pose, hips open enough for birthing twin barges down the Panama Canal. In my twenties I woke up and pretended that I was OK with upsetting people, like it was an ingrained trait. A fault in my personality – no, my DNA – that couldn't be changed. If you wanted to be my friend, an atom in my life, you had to succumb to my temperamental nucleus. You had to take the two drinks with the twenty, the rough with the smooth. But the roughness was like sliding belly-first across sandpaper that's been dusted with shards of broken mirror. Some people stuck it out, fucking hell, but the abrasiveness kept many more at arm's length. You never get close to sandpaper, you just get worn down.

Maybe I should go on an apology tour and atone for all those not-so-great behaviours. The time I hit two girls with a Christmas tree. The time I ripped someone's passport in half. The time I asked the PR running the press trip for a dick pic. The vases I've smashed. The close friends I've masturbated over. The G-A-Y bouncer I accused of being a racist (he wasn't). My husband is helping with this list, and it turns out he's much more easily embarrassed than me. He's suggested the time I walked over a car in London Fields at 4 p.m., 'over the bonnet and onto the roof'. He also mentioned the time I used a family barbecue as a UFO and sang the *X-Files* theme tune. All social *faux pas*, yes, but no real criminality. In fairness the most disappointing things I've done drunk involve being too loud or throwing up or drinking an entire tin of custard before bed. But upsetting people rankles. I believe a relationship is always salvageable – just look at my marriage in the aftermath of walking over the car – so I'll meet the previously offended one-on-one over soft drinks and Welsh rarebit. I will apologise. I will listen. They will feel heard.

We all have people we've wronged. It's human nature to bash up against each other. And I have been poison-chaliced with a personality type that *isn't* the one where you can't stop pleasing people. Most fallings-out end in some kind of stalemate, in a cul de sac where neither of you will compromise. A stalemate keeps us from swallowing our pride and saying sorry and lets us indignantly flounce off without too much crippling self-examination. During those fallings-out I tend to blinkeredly say, 'I'm not the type of person who [insert atypical, repeated personal behaviour].' I also say, 'But is she/he *really* happy though?', which you can say about anyone on the planet and never have to take a look at yourself.

The relationship that inevitably goes south is with your ex, who gets under your skin like it's a couture suit and knows where all the weak seams are. As a rule of thumb, it's unadvisable to get back with an ex, like returning to a fizzled-out firework. Walk away and don't turn back. Exes are easier to walk away from than siblings because nobody harbours resentment like a blood relative, but that's another story. Friendships have non-genetic boundaries that you can drunk-sandpaper down to nothing. Re-friending means excavating your feelings like Howard Carter, which is difficult over Welsh rarebit. It's much easier to bury the hatchet when you're drunk, because examining irresponsible actions is a sobering experience. It's too easy to mumble 'Sorry' through a fog of gin, because it feels good for you to say it and your inhibitions are at ground zero. Sober 'Sorry' is the macro nutrition of a good friendship. Sober 'Sorry' is a magic spell that turns the pumpkin of the feud into a beautiful carriage. Sober 'Sorry' is empathy. Not sorry for yourself, not sorry for your actions, but sorry for how that other person felt. Where drinking is an internalised experience, an adventure inside your own head, sobriety is coming home. Sobriety is empathy – thinking of other people without the interference of alcohol and its conjured desire for chips and burger sauce. Looking someone dead in the eye and being accountable without slurring your words. Sober 'Sorry' is human connection without distraction. A hard relate that's not being enhanced by two drinks. Sober 'Sorry'. Sober 'I fucked it up'. Sober 'I love you'. Sober comms is the closest to true love we can get because there's no interference with the signal. You can't rely on the inhibition-losing sleight of hand of alcohol. Forget whipping the tablecloth off a table, getting close to people without a drink in your hands is the real magic trick.

Treasures Untold

Like the suspicious 1969 moon-landing photos, or a push-up bra filled with chicken fillets, IKEA meatballs deceive you. On the glistening surface they're nothing but a harmless ball of beef, mere fuel for your IKEA sweep. But there's a familiar taste, slightly metallic, on the tip of your tongue. It tastes like the time you made a throwaway comment that made your mum cry. Or the early days of Twitter when you trolled Myleene Klass. Or the time you bought harem pants from House of Deréon. IKEA meatballs taste like regret. They taste like your shattered desires and reconstituted dreams. You see, the meatballs are the consolation prize of a long journey that started with the great expectations of how you're *meant* to live. Real life and actual budgets erode these aspirations, reducing them to the gelatinous bile on a meatball.

When you buy a house, building-society adverts tell you you're meant to feel exuberant and achingly cute like the film *Amélie*, all whimsical cutlery and jars of pennies magically filling up in the corner. I can tell you right now, you just feel depleted. After all the house-searching, and the house-finding, and offer-making, and negotiating, and surveying, and whole-house-packing, and man-with-a-van-ing, and new-keying, you just feel shattered. Drained like a once pus-filled boil. On that first night – after eating pizza straight from the box by candlelight and giving up on find-ing your toothbrush – you feel numb.

The night we moved into our house I thought we'd quickly bareback in the hallway and unpack within thirty-six hours and I'd be painting the second bedroom in dungarees by Christmas. That is not what happened. We drank Veuve Clicquot from some gross teacups we found in a cupboard. A little tipsy, I ripped down all the net curtains. I then tore up carpets and revealed rickety floorboards that are still exposed three years later. The little mushrooms of nail that dot the house like a Hansel and Gretel map still tear holes in your socks, and one once took out a pair of gum-soled Adidas trainers.

A little tip house-wise: don't take out what you can't afford to replace quickly. You end up with the shell of a house that's very echo-y and doesn't have adequate barriers between you and the sewer rats. I felt dead macho when I smashed the kitchen cabinets to smithereens, like the Incredible Hulk but with ballerina arms and a hammer. One free afternoon I kicked down the wall between the bathroom and a bedroom wearing the super-cheap Birkenstocks that don't have any cork bedding. Now we have an open-plan toilet upstairs, cavernous like the Batcave but painted magenta by whoever sold us the house. Stalagmites of house debris build up in a room that we agreed wouldn't be a junk room but now contains nothing but junk. Not long after the kitchen incident, our jar of pennies magically unfilled when we got a new roof and the price swelled like Violet Beauregarde chewing three-course gum. The last email from the roofer said: 'Sorry, but I'm not the one who bought an old house.' The worst thing about a new roof is that you walk around your house and it looks exactly the same; you have the same house with a new hat. After three months the whole transformative process plateaued, a teen movie paused during a crucial makeover montage. My dungarees remain unsplattered with paint.

For anyone who hasn't moved into a Mount Everest of a renovation, the actual furnishing of your house is what people like to call 'the fun part' because they're either cash-rich or time-rich or both. It's fairly easy to start a Pinterest board with cute pictures of a photographer's Manhattan loft and Alvar Aalto cocktail cabinets. Enjoy the honeymoon of picture research, pretend you're in Jamaica and getting laid every night and pin pictures to your boards like you're never coming back. Buy coffee-table books about pottery. Buy coffee-table books about brutalism. Buy coffee-table books about coffee tables. Buy that Entrance Halls of Milan book. And there must be a Phaidon book that celebrates marble. Buy anything that seems marble-focused. Leaf through eBay. Set an alert for *deco cabinets*. Paint swatch blobs of

Farrow & Ball on every wall like tea-tree oil on spotty teenage skin. Think big, then think bigger. Consider moving windows. And exterior walls. A super basement and a rooftop pool aren't extravagances, they're essential for living. Like Neil Armstrong on the moon, the first step is to subscribe to *House & Garden* and *Architectural Digest* and *Apartamento*. One small step for toilet reading, one giant leap for your humble *château*.

Magazines are bibles for living. Page after page of people you'll never be living lives you'll never have. Our feeds do the same but we're our own editors-in-chief, personally selecting our bespoke editorial team. We're watching a select group of people we'd like to be friends with talk about things that we're interested in. We're year 7s watching the year 9s in Wonderbras applying eyeshadow. Sometimes we contribute, sometimes we eavesdrop. Our feeds are couture, tailored to our personal interests, but like all great clothes they flatter the form. We are showcased the best of the lives we snoop. The cream atop the milk. A compilation of greatest hits. Now that's what I call Instagram. We're always looking at something overly romanced. We compare our own lives with the ones on the screen in our hand in a way that we don't when we're at the multiplex with a trough of popcorn and a vat of Diet Coke.

To covet is a natural human condition. We want possessions outside of what we can legitimately possess. That's one type of aspiration. Coveting is one of the reasons we have the word *steal* and the word *affair*. We all want what we can't have. If *The Silence of the Lambs* taught us more than how to harvest back-skin to tailor a suit, it's that we covet the things we see every day. Interiors magazines and accounts enable this behaviour, showing us a parallel world where people live carefree lives in tasteful surroundings, effortlessly knocking up a batch of pancakes for their 2.4 children. We become peeping Toms to their existences – artfully messy kitchen worktops, an aerial shot of a 'thrown-together' lunch, walnuts left on a Georgian staircase. Sometimes it's relatable couples laughing their way through a renovation, albeit in Bretons and holding oversized mugs of tea with two hands. Mainly we see the finished product: rustic bliss, pristine eclecticism, wall-to-wall good decisions. People have marble hearths and their chimneys swept, and matching fire-pokes for their open fires. I'll light the fire, you put the flowers in the vase that you bought today. They always have unlimited, appropriate flower vases or jugs, which is a level of domestic equilibrium that gives me a jealousy-induced nosebleed. They have a glut of lighting options. And little alabaster busts of heads that are probably distant relatives. And sparsely populated shelves. And paintings they did themselves in their studio at the bottom of the garden before ambling to the open-plan kitchen for a snack.

The question often becomes *How many wonders can one cavern hold?* Although we live in an interior-design war zone, I still fantasise about my pretentious bits, hidden away in storage boxes in the Batcave. The crocodile skin from South Africa that I smuggled back across international waters in my belt loops. A fish slice I bought from Margaret Howell when I was a student. A Campari ashtray even though I don't smoke because I want to keep my door keys in something quite Italian. My mum's Beatles songbook. My grandma's ceramic cabbage. We once asked ourselves *Which taps represent us as a couple?*, so there are two pairs of brass art deco faucets in a tote bag somewhere. We have a glut of male nudes – busts, drawings, paintings and photographs – and I'm considering banishing them all to the downstairs loo, rather than have homoeroticism confront you at every turn. Love isn't just about where you put your dick, it's about how you spend your evenings and weekends and how you plan a holiday and plot a future. The vacation crap you buy together and lug home is proof that you're in love. Literally tokens of affection. When you get back from a trip the tan fades but the trinkets linger.

Travel loot coupled with design classics also remind you that you're cultured and practical. You live with both utility and aesthetic reverence, with the boundaries of what things do and how they look fusing like conjoined carnival twins. Everything has meaning beyond its function in a complex ecosystem of interior charisma. All the stuff around you is a reflection of your taste, and your culture, and your achievements. A wall of books is key because you can literally spell out how cultured you are in bold, eclectic fonts on numerous spines. Your books are the cliff face of an intelligence mountain you've created and scaled, abseiling past Penguin Classics and Zadie Smiths. And books are the greatest thing on earth – until you have to move house. Many a disc has been slipped to a Picasso monograph.

I long to live in some kind of eclectic woke bohemia, with ancient nooks and crannies, modernist flourishes *and* underfloor heating. Somehow lived-in and layered in heritage but not annoyingly archaic. On paper this sounds like steampunk, but it is categorically not steampunk. All the windows being replaced by portholes is a desire for some unknown reason, which my architect (brother-in-law) has vetoed. In my head my home is a heady mix of the Bloomsbury group, hotels that coil round caged elevators, my mum's ex's house in France, the rugs at Sigmund Freud's, the apartment in *Green Card*, the coathooks at the ICA, a kitchen I KPed in as a teen, a lovingly restored art school, the corrugated aluminium at the Acropolis Museum, Poirot's London apartment, the attic bathrooms at 2 Willow Road, the abandoned penguin cage at London Zoo, dark rooms scalloped with booths that serve icy martinis, and anywhere they serve prawn cocktails in silver dishes.

Of course, you don't get that level of romanticism at IKEA. It's the Mecca of brazenly functional furniture with almost no backstory or hidden secrets – the opposite of an *EastEnders* family. IKEA sells zero-hours contracts of furniture: just do the job when I need you to, thanks, bye. And of course this works for *so many* people. Affordable, functional, accessible design. But affordable, functional and accessible are the antithesis of eclectic woke bohemia. It's difficult to picture Freud in a Malm bed. A prawn cocktail on an unbreakable IKEA plate is fine, but it doesn't whisper 'I got married at Rochelle Canteen,' does it?

IKEA is not just a bargain basement, it's all the floors above too, right up to the bargain loft conversion. What it lacks in romantic Frida Khalo's Mexican home aesthetic, it makes up for in sheer bargainness. After you start to cost up your Pinterest board of dreams, your financial house of cards collapses. Your dreams are rubble like the mini mountains in my junk room waiting for next bank holiday's trip to the tip. But your wall of books still needs an infrastructure. You still need shelving. This is what brings you to IKEA on a Saturday afternoon, reconciled to affordable versions of the board. You're disappointed, like when you see a hot guy at the pool, with broad shoulders and abs, but he puts on horrible pants.

At IKEA there's no Vitra, no Aalto, no Starck. But there are plenty of lookalikes. Every aspect of the IKEA experience is you trying to make your life look like someone else's. You sit in the long shadow cast by a Bauhaus-type lamp, or the residual heat of an Ernö Goldfinger-esque towel rail. And it's a bounty of stuff, like the haul carried off by the rabble of old men who robbed that safe-deposit place in Hatton Garden, but it's decidedly unprecious. Tat in the form of taps, tea sets and TV tables. There are multi-functional desks, bumper packs of napkins and wire baskets of bath sponges. It's an Aladin's cave with considerably more lamps, all of which are LED and will outburn the sun.

Most annoyingly, it's impossible to replace bad furniture. Like a butt plug, once it's in it's not going anywhere. A Billy bookcase is an undesirable tenant you can't be bothered to evict. Each cheese grater and laundry basket and bedside table sits around being unchangingly tolerable, lying dormant like Vesuvius. No eruption. No rapture. No deliverance.

IKEA isn't just for the newly disappointed. Adequate lives call for adequate measures, and as a couple there's always a reason to nip to IKEA. A visit to the store is an attempt to *feng shui* your relationship. To find pragmatic solutions to the labours of co-habitual love. To reignite the fires of passion with a spark of joy only achievable though a raffia rug and its latent promise of a carpet burn. Sailing through a tempest of MDF and passive-aggressive comments, IKEA's veteran couples revisit arguments past. A silent war like the one you have in your office over what's playing on the Sonos. Rehashing previous trips. The time you were in a rush before that birthday barbecue. The time you both got lost. The time you deliberately got lost in retaliation for the time you both got lost but you know he did it on purpose. The time your fella said something innocuous about the kitchen blind and you overreacted and unleashed a torrent of pent-up anger, citing multiple incidents of perceived injustice including but not exclusive to the way his mum talked to you that one time at dinner.

Disappointment is a wound. Once all the joy has left your body (somewhere near the home office section), staunch the bleeding with reasonably-priced solutions. Re-energise with meatballs. Take your regrets, mince them, add an egg and some breadcrumbs. Ease the sense of anti-climax. Every time you feel regret, bite into an IKEA meatball. Not able to afford the dream apartment in the perfect location location location? Bite. Didn't agree on a wall colour? Bite. Only in this relationship because it failed with 'the one'? Bite. If you can't be with the one you love, love the one you're with.

You're not alone. There are queues of other couples, all their faces frozen in smiles that imply relief. Job done. We survived IKEA. But everyone is bereft, mourning the life they can't afford. Obviously there is one expensive-looking woman in the queue. A touch too thin and kitting out her holiday home in St Ives. She's bulk-buying forgettable kitchen bits in materials that wipe down easily and won't shatter when dropped. She's paying with an AmEx. A plague on both her houses.

The fairytales we're read as kids don't factor in the harsh reality of late capitalism. The futures they lead us to dream up don't include passive-aggressively queueing in IKEA on a Saturday afternoon with a trolley full of Snow White matt emulsion and a Little Red Extractor Hood. Fantasy is whittled away to leave a thin skewer of reality. The princess and the allen key. Goldilocks and the three chairs.

It's not snobbery, this IKEA comedown. It's just not what you planned for your life. It's our disenchanted commonality. You don't pursue the meatballs, you end up with them, in the same way you don't pursue a house in the suburbs. IKEA always feels like a stepping stone, rather than a destination. A drive-thru on the way to a modernist Bloomsbury nirvana, with well-sourced rugs. Meatballs are a digestible consolation prize, bouncing around your stomach like the bombs from the Dam Busters. They're the kind of nourishment you got during rationing, when nobody ate gourmet but they were super-healthy. And though you should never turn your nose up at a decent source of protein, it's hard to stomach the experience. The taste of regret still lingers. My favourite hobby is talking shit about someone for an extended time and then ending my rant with, 'But I love her, she's like my best friend.' But I love IKEA, she's like my best friend.

Fifty Ways to Leave Your Lover

Preface: *The first draft of this chapter had a whole chunk about how much I love my husband, but it was so soppily good I shifted it to its own chapter, which he'll read and then cry and then realise that us finding each other was written in the stars. What remains here makes it sound as if being single is my preferred status and I think being coupled is a massive drain on your resources as a human. Being coupled is a massive drain on your resources, but that's the fun of it. Enjoy.*

Madonna was right: Life is a mystery, everyone must stand alone. Being coupled up is like being happy but splitting the happiness down the middle like a large electricity bill. You're literally half-hearted, sharing joint custody of your own emotions with another person. Love is half an orgasm. Love is stabbing out one eye. It's half a club sandwich, three slices of bread and no chicken or bacon or mayo. Love is having 50 per cent of your dreams fulfilled, which sounds like a lot but you wind up sitting bolt upright in bed in a cold sweat and realising you only have half the duvet.

You and your partner are co-dependent barnacles suckered to each other, with no light getting in. Cake is great because the sponge layers happily cohabit, separated by an amicable squirt of cream and jam. Human union is the same slices of spongecake, but with no moist faultline of filling or icing, just dense sponge all the way down to the plate. You're never really home alone – someone else's recent, invisible presence is a dew that drenches everything. He's a poltergeist homing in on what you need and moving it somewhere out of sight. Your door keys. Your passport. Your sense of self. The rational parts of you disappear like the four distinct seasons after climate change is done. You have to constantly check in and you feel guilty if you don't, like when I was fifteen and I went to a festival and I didn't call my mum for three days. When you're married you can't book a dinner or flights or even do a casual retweet without some consultation. Incels have got it so, so wrong. Sharing orifices with another person is grim, and then you have to fill the long expanses of white noise between orgasms.

Love holds you back like reins on a thoroughbred horse. You don't need a man in the same way you don't need two kidneys. You don't even need a best friend. Thelma *sans* Louise. Britney's first marriage, much like her Vegas residency, taught us that love is a transient performance, over in less time than you spent on your last Instagram post. Her K-Fed second marriage taught us that love is only manageable if you smoke a bunch of weed and never connect with real emotions, which actually feels more feasible. We don't need no piece of paper from the city hall keeping us tied and true. Marriage is like matt-painting a pearl – you hide its lustre. Or you end up sacrificially lacquering your partner and dulling your own shine. Somebody always gets eclipsed. This is a fact. Of course I'll come to your summer wedding dressed to the nines and I'll Cheshire cat smile, but I'll be quietly thinking *Another one in the casket*. I'll dress the part, shake the mother of the bride's hand as crocodile tears roll down my cheeks. I'll squeal when the bouquet comes out, but my best man's speech will be short: *I have never in my life yelled at a girl like this. I was rooting for you. We were all rooting for you.*

Single people are great on their own: they don't need any additions, like a phone that doesn't need apps. Solitude is its own gift. Free from the shackles of another person you can have it all. All the thinking time. All the reading time. None of the noise or emotional labour. Solitude is an own goal where the only team playing takes the cup. You're a one-person band like Bert in *Mary Poppins*. You can board a train, dressed like a sliver of night sky, without a destination in mind. You can talk to other passengers. Or not. The world is your oyster, no, a dozen oysters, and you don't have to give six to your husband. Imagine *Eat Pray Love* about a couple and it repositions as an insufferable fable of show-offs posting their Italian pizza on Instagram.

Marriage leaves little room for adventurous and international jaunts. It is our collective Achilles heel, keeping us grounded on *terra firma*, away from adventure in the great wide somewhere. One day you'll fly away, leave all this to yesterday – but have you ever seen two birds flying together holding hands? Bette Midler's 'Wind Beneath My Wings' is a fallacy, because wind bumps the vessel and terrifies the captive passengers. Your partner is the turbulence. This is how collarbones get broken. It's impossible to maintain upward thrust as a pair. Things only went wrong for Icarus because he got cocky. Rather than *Don't fly*, the lesson here is *Don't fly too close to the sun*. Independence is singularity. Freedom's just another word for nothing left to lose. If you've already Velcroed yourself to another person it's time to disengage.

Severing any relationship leaves you beautiful and detached like Gwyneth's head in the box at the end of *Se7en*. This is a good thing. It's a palate-cleanser, leaving you free to do you without compromise. Book an express ticket to singledom and take your revenge body for a spin. Do not quietly annul the marriage. Here are fifty ways to cut the cord.

1. If the cord is organic and twiny like Tarzan's vine, have a thousand rats gnaw at it until it breaks. If the cord is built of sturdier stuff try a hacksaw. I heard about a guy who had a titanium cock ring stuck on his penis for three days because the allen key threaded. If the cord of love attaching you is made of titanium be prepared to lose appendages on the wrong side of the knot. Liberty is a form of sacrifice.

2. Tell him you've been alive too long to stay in love with him. Romeo and Juliet are the blueprint of romantic love, but life expectancy for Elizabethans was forty-two. Eternal love is only doable if you die before fifty. Modern life expectancy and the eradication of the black death isn't a reason to stay together. The Capulets were only in it for the transference of property.

3. Tell him you've been trying to get into him like when you were trying to get into jazz. Or watercolours. Or crochet. Or anal. Unused things tend to end up stuffed at the back of a drawer gathering dust. Your relationship is a spiraliser.

4. Ghost him. Not in the without-a-trace millennial way. More like Patrick Swayze and Demi Moore. Hire Whoopi Goldberg as a go-between. Solve a crime, avenge your death even, but eventually transcend to the celestial realm.

5. Have face-altering surgery so you're unrecognisable to him and steal away on a glamorous steam train (preferably trans-Siberian), leaving only a whiff of your signature scent on your pillow. When summer comes, start a new life in a new town where nobody knows your name, in a climate where everybody's forehead glistens and they smell ripe. Wear outrageous ensembles that your mother would call tarty. Own it.

6. Have a surgeon do a real-life face swap and leave *as* him. It's not me, it's me. This is quite painful physically, but deliciously meta.

7. Develop a brand partnership and call a big yellow branded Uber to take away your old man. Don't it always seem to go that you don't know what you've got till it's #spon.

8. Tell him you're a horse-whisperer but he's a deaf horse. Boxer in *Animal Farm* is loyal and hard-working, but he still ends up at the knacker's yard. Clarify that he is Boxer and you are the pigs running the show.

9. Get a close friend to set a honey trap, seducing him over mid-morning coffee, pressed up against the kitchen island. If he doesn't bite, call in those terrifying Cock Destroyer women. They'll finish him off.

10. Have him *faux*-kidnapped by a biker gang. No idea how you find a biker gang. Alternatively have a friend dress as an adult version of the Child Catcher from *Chitty Chitty Bang Bang*, and lure him in with the greatest bait known to man: quality podcasts. They'll take him away in a cage on wheels. Pray Dick van Dyke doesn't perform a rescue.

11. Tell him that comparing something to the size of a football pitch is grounds for divorce.

12. Tell him tomato ketchup with a roast dinner is sacrilege.

13. Tell him he's sweet, but who wants diabetes?
14. Tell him you've searched your soul but you could never really give your full self to someone still using Android.
15. Tell him he never let you get the eight hours' sleep needed for true happiness. And that his skincare regime gives you anxiety. His skin's his biggest organ, a barrier holding things in *and* out, and it needs due care. His approach to moisturiser is laughable.
16. Tell him he inhibited your happiness like the stuff they pump into your heart when you overdose on opioids.
17. Tell him the relationship was a crisp kimchi but now it's fetid fizzy cabbage which Goop is interested in rebranding as Magic Greens but it's too late for the relationship. Flirting with salmonella is wellness.
18. Apply for the Jane McDonald vacancy on a Caribbean cruise because you've always had this crazy dream of singing all the classical roles aboard a ship before you're twenty-one. The chance to sing *Les Mis* in international waters is an unmissable opportunity. Remind him you're a solo act.
19. Say you did the Ancestry blood test and you think you're cousins. Or the twins from *The Parent Trap*. When he asks how you got his DNA, act dumb.
20. Sew prawns into the hem of a curtain and leave on olfactory grounds.

21. Get a Katharine Hamnett T-shirt that says '50% of this relationship wants out'.

22. Tell him it's your anniversary today and you can't believe he forgot something so important. It doesn't matter what the actual anniversary is. Say it's the centenary of the first time you wore culottes in front of him. If he quibbles, gaslight him.

23. Mute him like the old school friends on Instagram you have nothing in common with. This means still living with him but never acknowledging any of his comments or stories.

24. Leave a series of scribbly notes like the guy with the hook in *I Know What You Did Last Summer*. The notes should smell of fish guts and blood. Freak him out until he confesses to something, anything, and then ask him to leave.

25. Introduce him to Scientology. Wait.

26. Having an affair is dead *passé* and predictable. People always fuck the gardener. Consider real gardening instead. Smuggle your possessions out in a wheelbarrow under rolls of turf.

27. Slowly diminish him, like a bar of soap getting worn to a nub.

28. Slowly diminish yourself until he thinks he's too good for you. Slowly wring out the romance like a damp flannel until all that's left is a whiffy coil of cotton.

29. Tell him your relationship is the Fyre Festival, all fart and no shit.
30. Tell him your relationship is an eight-hour meeting that could've been an email.
31. Don't go to therapy, just overshare on your timeline until his mates see.
32. Get drunk at a dinner party with close friends and a few choice strangers and talk in detail about your sex life and how he closes his eyes during penetration. Phrase everything as jokey but look people dead in the eye with tears welling but never falling.
33. Ditto at his family's Christmas get-together.
34. Disguise yourself with face paint like one of those annoying performance people who paint themselves to look like the background of an image. Wait until he stops searching for you. This could take years.
35. Fake an apocalypse like the air-raid experience at the Imperial War Museum. Have an MP3 of apocalypse sounds playing as you bundle him into a shelter at 4 a.m. Leave him in the trench downing cans of beans. Tell people he's moved to the Bahamas.
36. Tell him the tuxedo didn't make him look like James Bond. Tell him that magazines saying any medium-famous guy in a tux 'might be the new Bond' is just a way to sell suits and watches. Tell him you never liked the watch. The watch always looked cheap.

37. Tell him his underwear is gross. That you tried to see past it but you're not a miracle worker. Tell him it's too late for new boxer-briefs. The relationship is threadbare like his pants.
38. Send him all the fag ash from a house party with a note saying you've been cremated and don't cry for me I'm already dead.
39. Have Alan Sugar record a personal You're Fired YouTube video and post it on his Facebook wall.
40. Tell him you're Britain and he's Europe.
41. Tell him you're Geri and he's the Spice Girls. Tell him he's the two members of Destiny's Child that got replaced by Michelle.
42. Tell him he was your cup of tea but you drink champagne now.
43. Tell him he's the yolk but you're making meringue.
44. Tell him he was your type on paper but everything's digital now.
45. Tell him you're both the same end of the magnet.
46. Tell him he's a tasty snack but you need a whole meal. You needed a vitamin-supplement chaser after every interaction with him. That's not sustenance.
47. Tell him your true calling is getting the *Sex and the City* third film made and, like a Knight of the Round Table on a crusade, you cannot rest until it's in production. Reconciliation between Sarah Jessica Parker and Kim Cattrall is more than a vocation. It's who you are.

48. Blame tarot, or homeopathy, or osteopathy. Say you found yourself at City Yoga or Pilates or Barry's Bootcamp.
49. Tell him you always knew it was doomed but also that you never had the slightest inkling.
50. Remind him he's lucky his breasts are small and humble, soft peaks as it were, and he has time to re-mate.

Penis Poirot

I feel so lonely when people talk about cars. All the makes and models have familiar names but they don't *mean* anything. I understand the concept of horsepower, but not the measure of it or its real-world application. I can't work out how anybody absorbs all that information and stores it away, whipping it out at the pub after a pint. An automotive reservoir in their head that they can drag for exacting asides and say chassis without batting an eyelid. I remember faces, not names, like the prostitute in *Bugsy Malone*. I feel the same about dogs, and how people can point out different breeds without their phone. I don't give a Shih Tzu. It's the same with trees, where I only know silver birch and conker. And with wine I enjoy a nice Sancerre, but I never keep notes in my head outside of 'dry and white', which coincidentally describes all my exes.

When I was younger I had the same reaction when boys talked about girls. I understood how women looked, their form, their function, their warm nether regions, but this didn't stir anything in me. I had no desire to explore women, to work them out or give them pleasure. Priority boarding was not an aspiration. Mucking in with the lads wasn't an option. My sexuality was still very much a gelatinous blob, magma cooling on the surface, but even then I knew I was different. I didn't know I liked men, exactly. I just knew I didn't like women *like that*. I had no drive to learn more. Women were like cars: lots of moving parts that didn't interest me.

The first half of secondary school is a time before you have any real sexuality, before your hormones kick in and you get body hair and pendulum mood-swings. My gayness registered as a sort of low-level hum of manageable discomfort, like my underwear was on inside out. My desire for men came in slowly, like global warming, and just made a kind of ebbing, lazy sense. I never had a lightbulb moment, my dick pointing towards men like a compass finding north or some colossal magnetic pull towards their multiple orifices. In those fledgling years I became immediately introspective, a penis Poirot observing the suspect (me), but I don't mean wanking. Like any sleuth, I was gathering evidence to be meticulously examined behind closed doors. Taking notes on each passing cloud of desire. Inspecting every dick pang. Deciphering my real attractions versus the red herrings. I was slowly deducing the mechanics of men themselves and becoming a scholar of the way they moved and talked and interacted. A claustrophobic whodunit of non-conforming arousal. The suspense was murder, but there were no arrests because there was no felon. Was I even culpable for my feelings? In retrospect, it's an easily solvable mystery: I was sailing at a rate of knots towards full homosexual. But at thirteen I hadn't a clue of the closing scene. The final destination was unknown, so like a surprise birthday trip, I sat back and gazed out the window with trepidation.

I remember revolutions of uncertainty. I can't be gay because I want a family. I can't be gay because I masturbated over a picture of boobs. I can't be gay because I'm indifferent to women, rather than repulsed by them. Maybe it's a phase? Maybe I can text 'STOP' to opt out? Maybe I can delete this gay app from my personal iOS. Like a decent sourdough loaf, my sexuality proved in the dark, creeping up my insides until I was full to the brim with it. I looked like everyone else, but my innards were made up differently, like I'd ingested my gay twin in the womb and he was alive and well and wearing me as a heterosexual skin, literally a straight-jacket. I played along, adopting placebos of straightness – reading *Loaded* magazine, wearing baggy jeans and spraying Lynx on my pits. I spoke in a slightly deeper voice and adopted a completely unflourished walk. A performance piece of heteronormal activity. As a tall, loud, brown adolescent I always stood out, but I wanted desperately to disappear from your line of vision. To mingle. To pass. I was desperate to be the right kind of standout. Like a goth. Not a gay. Teenage girls are pack animals, and teenage boys can sniff out femininity like sharks in water. I didn't want to give anyone the scent. Incidentally, a great way to signal your difference as a young gay is to say you don't like football. Out loud.

The realisation, when it dropped, was obvious: women are great but I don't fancy them. Somewhere over the rainbow my gay forefathers – Oscar Wilde, Harvey Milk, Michelangelo – gathered in heaven to toast me with pina coladas with sparklers. It's worth mentioning here the things that turned me gay, in case you slip as well: My Little Pony, t.A.T.u., Friedrich von Trapp, the pool scene in *Cruel Intentions*, gender-neutral Kinder Surprise, making a cushion cover in DT, Japanese toilets that douche your arse, Anna Friel's lesbian kiss on *Brookside*.

Like trees, there are subdivisions of gay men – bears and daddies and ones that dress like Mr Toad of Toad Hall and collect antiques. Some are just slabs of muscle that press against you in the dark of a club. Some are covered in piercings like the hull of the *Titanic*, ready to take you straight to the bottom. Some are wispy little Quentin Blake etchings that float away if you blow them too hard and some are voluptuous Ursulas from *The Little Mermaid*, but with two legs. I've never had a type, but I've never been a type either, which I tell myself is a kind of superpower in the same way David Hockney has never been a painter synonymous with any particular art movement. I'm the David Hockney of gays, unboxable, like an oddly-shaped vase at the John Lewis Christmas wrapping counter. I'm impossible to overlook, but not really what you're looking for. I would be terrible on *Love Island* because nobody's type is tall, loud, needy black guys who keep asking you what you're thinking.

I'm not tattooed. I'm not muscular. I have one vanilla piercing. I'm not the kind of rich you marry for the shoes and holidays. I'm not the kind of nice you marry because you've had it up to here with bad boys. I'm not the kind of handsome that drenches knickers. I'm not a chiselled, aloof doctor in a Mills & Boon that you emotionally erode over 256 pages. I have no gimmicks with which to woo. No pick-up lines. No tricks. Nothing up my sleeve. Some gays prefer sleeveless shirts anyway. Shirtless gay is its own type. And regardless of type, gay men have traditional gay things, the same way straight people have Coachella or boot-cut jeans. The rainbow is an obvious one – oft seen in the window of your quiet neighbours who exclusively wear polo shirts and listen to Bach – but there's more. Iced coffee. Switching off read recipes. Putting your phone face-down at family events. Going on dates and not knowing if it's a date. Going on Antoni from *Queer Eye*'s feed and getting immediately irrationally jealangry. Portmanteaus like jealangry. Working out if someone's gay in three scrolls on Instagram. Commenting just the flame emoji on pictures. Commenting *dead* on pictures. Liking all of the pictures where the guy you like has his top *on*. Sliding into his DMs with the flame emoji. Being a twink, which is a nascent gay. Twinks going blond when they turn twenty-five before they evolve into otters. Otters evolving into bears. Calling people daddy. Gay brunch, which is normal brunch but the pancakes are made with protein powder. Protein powder. Protein shakes. Egg whites. Leg day. *Brokeback Mountain*. Turtlenecks. Short shorts. Turtlenecks with short shorts. Fancying side-kick characters like Harvey from *Sabrina*. Fancying most straight guys. Dressing like most straight guys. Saying you hate straight guys. Pretending to be happy on Instagram. Pretending to be depressed on Twitter. Poppers. Saying you hate poppers. Grindr. Saying you hate Grindr.

So the teenage me knew I was homosexual. Not that I told anyone. Post-epiphany I became uncharacteristically quiet, withdrawing into myself like a garlicky escargot. I slept a lot. My mum thought I might be anaemic. The doctor said I was just tired. In a way I rolled a condom onto my heart, a 99.9 per cent effective barrier against showing any emotion. Ribbed for nobody's pleasure. I did not follow my desire to its natural conclusion. The Pied Piper of my lust played floor fillers and I shuffled on the sidelines. Great literature, with its sense and sensibility, promises you a dramatic life of secret love and yearning and passionate kisses in the pouring rain, but I was too scared to pen the first sentence. My dissertation on love remained unwritten. I spent night after night at home in my room. I wrote Joni Mitchell's saddest bangers on my wall in purple Berol, and dreamed of the kind of love she sang about, with someone to drink a case of me. I looked in the mirror a bunch, too. I lacked velvet rage, and the crippling shame of gayness I later read about. I just projected all my feelings inwards. I tried to stay introverted, but something always seeped through the cracks. I can't mope for shit. I can't dwell. I tried to be properly depressed, but like Louis Vuitton knockoffs on eBay, it didn't really fit. My weapons-grade sass always shone through.

OK, I had no friends, which sounds terrible and I'm sure it was at the time. But I remember it as a fact, without any desperate emotion attached. Up until that point I'd always been popular because I never knew what shyness was. And the no-friend era was a dip, like a car radio going through a tunnel. It's a closed chapter I don't bother to reread because I don't recognise myself as a confused, inactive victim of my circumstances. Part of what makes me fearless now is the years of being fearful. I don't want to harp on like every other extrovert who has to keep telling you they're an intro-vert, but without friends I spent masses of time alone inside my own head, truly believing all romantics meet the same fate someday, cynical and drunk and boring someone in some dark café.

In retrospect the whole thing was fortifying – all the self-reflection built up layers of self-understanding that are now part of my buoyant, if not slightly annoying, self-assur-ance. Also, that lone-wolf disposition has stayed with me. I still crave solitude as much as I love a gab. But I would never settle with someone for the sake of company. I don't need people, I choose them. It's the highest compliment.

At fifteen I accidentally watched an episode of *Queer as Folk* with my mum. The one where the schoolboy sucks off Aidan Gillen in his bedroom. She said, 'I think this might be too adult for you.' At fifteen I came out to her on the phone, sort of by accident, and my straight-acting house of cards toppled quite easily, because the foundations were already bent. Somehow you're saying to your mum you love dick, even though you've never experienced it. It's not about love at fifteen, is it? It's about your gonads. Knowing how to hide the sausage in theory, but never actually having hidden it. The closet is a funny place. Imagine being drunk but pretending not to be as tell-tale signals slip out. That's being in the closet. Acting normal as you reach boiling point within. Before I came out I'd been trying to keep a lid on myself and my voice and my mannerisms. My personality was dehydrated like space food, or the ghosts when they nearly die again at the end of *Beetlejuice*. The second I came out my whole personality reinflated like a party balloon. The instant I told someone I was gay I was able to just *be*. Not be myself, because I hadn't completely disappeared. But I could exist without concealment. I could interact without hiding some key part of myself.

In the closet I was a spiceless dal, but I emerged as a vindaloo in a cableknit under a magnifying glass on a summer's day. A side of pilau rice, a Peshwari naan and two Cobra beers and fuck it let's have a gulaab jamun and get an Uber home and feel each other up. I was *al dente* pasta with more bite. I felt like I'd been locked up tight for a century of lonely nights. My currency among the gays was newness. I was a resumé ready to be typed. I was a newly minted gay in the gay metropolis of Brighton, dipping my toe into the gayest things. I was on my way to fuck knows where, but being a directionless teenage drunk is its own thrill. I was pristine. A rolling stone yet to gather a single clump of moss. I had no concept of a desk job, or a mortgage, I was just guzzling up new experiences. Pouring myself a cup of ambition. Trying to get into clubs. Trying to get into politics. Trying to get into olives. I never worried I'd go stale one day like crisps left on the side after a house party. I was running on a battery life of unlimited future.

The vinegar stokes of the nineties were really something. *Big Brother* was still a social experiment, rather than a fame generator, and you could legitimately talk about the contestants like they were summer acquaintances. Gwyneth was still friends with Madonna, before all the Kabbalah and Goop, and they were papped in workout-wear with teensy veiny arms. We called it workout-wear because athleisure hadn't been invented. People still listened to Travis. Not even that. It was cool to listen to Travis. There were internet cafés and the aural assault of dial-up internet before MSN chats. Somebody else scanned your shopping for you at the supermarket. Nobody vaped. Nobody had ever said the word Tinder outside of an open-fire context. If you wanted to be thinner you went on a diet, because we hadn't rebranded starvation as wellness.

If, like me, you were a fledgling gay and you wanted attention there was a clear process. You got dressed up, left the house, queued for a club, queued for the coat check, queued for the bar and danced so everybody was watching, giving off the nonchalant air of someone who didn't make an effort at any one of these stages. We were all waiting for tonight. We had 'going-out' tops specifically for going out. You wouldn't wear them in the day. Ever. The walk of shame home loses its badge of dishonour in daywear. Design-wise, going-out tops left as little as possible to the imagination. Forever 'a bit clingy'. Never altogether comfortable. They exaggerated your shape – a push-up underwire system for women, pec-skimming for men – to serve up your body on a sexy platter of fabric, with wiggle room to dance the night away without chaffing. Each era has its defining going-out top. My epoch was marked by women in halterneck hand-kerchiefs tied at the back, matched with pornographically low-cut jeans or a sarong that dragged on the dirty club floor.

Being nineteen was the best year of my life. I had masses of independence and no real responsibilities. I stank of CK One and my biggest concern was waiting too long to masturbate before my parents came home. I got repetitive strain injury from playing Snake on my Nokia. I went out every night, and came home to a Mum-stocked fridge. I ate absolute shit but my body always looked nineteen. Devouring Pizza Express American Hots from the freezer. More spicy than a hot tamale. More meaty than Jon Hamm's crotch. I made hideous artery-clogging milkshakes of blitzed Mars ice creams and single cream. I must have been deeply self-conscious, like every other post-adolescent, but I don't really remember my body at all, apart from that it could now orgasm. I once shat myself to a Junior Senior song, aerobically dancing with myself in my room. I don't remember any other efforts to exercise.

Like Ancient Greece my pursuits were purely hedonistic, chasing down rock-hard pillars rather than Aphrodites. We were a LimeWire generation downloading free MP3s and listening to a lot of UK garage. A Craig David lifestyle was a non-ironic aspiration because he hadn't been ruined by Avid Merrion yet. Aiya Napa was a thing. Relationships were measured in bases. I've noticed you around, I find you very attractive. I was naturally nimble, unlike now when my spine is sphinx posed into flexibility, like forced taps on a bath. I didn't have a bunch of sex, but the promise of it was enough. Sex on the cusp of adulthood isn't that great: like a puppy humping your leg it's incredibly enthusiastic but stylistically lacks form. Like when two bottoms hook up and one of them tries to top. We would have to go to clubs to physically brush up against each other. Flesh all a-mesh. Static electricity. We drank snakebite and black because giving up sugar was not a thing. We sang 'Don't Call Me Baby', but it was a lie. People would say things like 'slag' and 'tranny' and 'faggot', because gender was completely fucked. You didn't get digitally poked. You got off with people. People kissed you in the street outside foam parties. You met people and didn't know what would happen next. People didn't come with nifty bios. Side note for the guys on apps who say 'no kissing': fix your heart. But in the nineties there were no spoilers. No DMs. There were the guys you let hit it and never call you again. That was the point. There were guys who thought spitting on it counts as foreplay. They were wrong. There were guys everywhere, because you had to go out to meet anybody, let alone *the one*. There was an air of possibility as you entered a club or afterparty. People were tired from dancing all night, not jaded from ruthless Tinder swiping.

Shall I compare thee to a summer's gay? I later spent years searching the globe for mean men to project my feelings onto, but it was a perfect summer, a mosquito frozen in the amber of UK garage before The Strokes came along and I took in all my jeans. I hope you had a similarly wasted summer in your youth. Not a summer of love, but of garish, cack-handed attempts at it. When every song on the radio was written specifically for you, when you were young and your heart was an open book. If this ain't love, why does it feel so good?

Gays for Theresa

If it was 1066 and I lived in Bayeux, they would sew an intricate tapestry depicting the nightly battles between me and my cat as we war over his dinner. My husband and I don't have kids or flatmates, so at one of our svelte house meetings we agreed to give the cat a single cup of dry food – chickeny biscuits. The cat wants the wet salmony sachets he's had before, but salmony sachets have to be rationed because of their salt content, and their ungodly expense, and their smell (going into him and coming out). Salmony doesn't give you a glossy coat, or strong bones, or free-falling stools. There's a whole matrix of micro-decisions that have led up to chickeny biscuits, including the constant impulse to purchase cat goods with 'Vitality' emblazed across them. Also, a catsitter once explained that the previous food I was feeding the cat was 'McDonald's for cats', and said, 'You could live off McDonald's too, but not for a long time.'

So each night a tragic tinkle of dry food cascades into the cat's bowl and echoes round the kitchen. His disappointment is palpable, quickly followed by a *You're joking, surely* stare – the look I expect my future kids to give me when they get a learning-focused gift for Christmas. The garnish of a single prawn can sometimes run effective diversion: he'll eat the prawn and accidentally munch all the way to the bottom of the bowl. If we don't have prawns there's a kitchen standoff, the three of us like that scene in *The Good, the Bad and the Ugly*, standing like statues, each waiting for the other to make the first move. The air is thick with *faux* chicken smell. Will he just eat the meal? Or will we cave in and give him half a salmony sachet? More often than not my husband caves. Our personal Bayeux tapestry would depict me clutching an arrow of chicken to my eye, or a prawn if we had any. I retreat to our bed preparing to sleep under the insulation of moulted cat hair from the beast's day of lounging. I feel guilt. Nothing is as sad as when I read that scruffing my cat was emasculating for him, and though I stopped immediately I still want to make those emasculating kitten years up to him. That doesn't mean a lifetime of bad food though. At Waterloo my husband did surrender.

Unlike our kitchen nightmare, military wars are a bit more tense. Is there anything less fun than real war? The civilian life-and-death jeopardy is exhausting. Drone strikes are a killjoy. Because of the chickeny/salmony standoff I'm empathetic to national leaders dealing with an enemy that won't take no for an answer. I'm sure the war bunker at the height of battle is acutely stressful, but I do think there's space for a little more attention sartorially. While you're signing off a chemical attack, could your legs look longer?

Or your shoulders broader? Does your shirt clash with the desk? The right cufflinks could really bring out the red of the nuke button.

Male prime ministers have it easy. They're able to play real-life Battleships without anyone commenting on their appearance, because they wear the most boring thing on the planet: a suit. A ubiquitous look for white guys in power, as commonplace in Westminster as diddling your expenses. A suit also never draws attention to the wearer: it's invisible, but not in an emperor's new clothes way. In the same way the hot bods of reality TV contestants create a chiselled level playing field, suits are camouflage so people can focus on business. The fun to be had out of a suit is boundless: see Grayson Perry's inclination towards a less traditionally masculine silhouette.

It's unlikely Justin Timberlake had Tony Blair in mind when he penned 'Suit & Tie', but he may as well have, such is the ease of political power dressing. Preparing to leave Number 10 in the morning must be a cinch. Do I have my navy suit? Are my shoes shiny? Is this tie party-coloured? Like an underground lair, suits are better off a bit dingy and lived-in, rather than attempting flamboyance. Whatever flourish a prime minister uses to accentuate his suit is lauded as distinct and iconic: Churchill's bowler hat (yawn), or Justin Trudeau's *Star Wars* socks (a yawn far, far away). David Cameron's rolling up of his sleeves as a metaphorical and physical manifestation of his readiness during his re-election campaign was thuddingly literal, cartoonish to the point of patronising. It's mortifying when *The Apprentice* wannabes – junior power-dressers – lug their wheelie suitcase across the Millennium Bridge in a turquoise suit with paisley lapels and half of Kew Gardens in the buttonhole. A suit is a bit like a soufflé: don't fiddle with it or the whole thing collapses.

Female prime ministers don't get the luxury of wearing an invisible suit. They have to wear dresses and skirts and little *ensembles* and be groomed and neat. We scrutinise them – with the beady eyes of a cat watching fake salmon pour from a foil sachet – expecting them to dress 'appropriately', based on a billion fashion micro-expressions: form, fit, flesh on view. Variations in skirt length speak volumes, and then there's the cardinal sin of a woman *not* dressing her age. Margaret Thatcher's clothes were dissected, from her fondness for Conservative (with a big C) blue to her oddly coquettish pussy-bow blouses, like a well-wrapped present, inside which is the demonisation of the working class and union warfare. A Kinder Surprise full of maggots. A Tiffany box containing a dog turd. Theresa May was repeatedly rinsed like fast-drying nylon. Her leopard-print kitten heels, expensive leather trousers and hostile accessories captured attention. Her daywear necklaces were all heavy-looking exaggerated chain, borrowed from Mr T. She was Britain's chained albatross, tethered to an isle that didn't want her, an unelected burden that felt like a curse. It's a sad state of affairs when the biggest distraction from running the country is a pair of rawhide slacks. But we couldn't overlook her fashion choices, because they signified her unrelatability. Could something have been done to make May seem more approachable? More normal? More like us? What might have been the catalyst to transform Theresa Maybe into Theresa Definitely? As the prime minister who built a coalition with a Northern Irish party that could be described as anti-homosexuality, it's ironic that Theresa could have found salvation in five gay men. We should have *Queer Eye*d Theresa May.

Are gay men inherently more tasteful? Do they take better care of themselves? Are they funnier and more engaged? Are they fountains of empathy and self-help? Do they dress better? The original *Queer Eye* in 2003 was created as a Frankensteinian cut-and-shut of TV shows: *What Not to Wear*; *How Clean is Your House?*; *Ready Steady Cook*. Five gay men would tsunami through a straight guy's life, douching his wardrobe, skincare and personality. The resurrected Netflix series has been tearing contemporary TV a new arsehole as the five presenters stand on the shoulders of gay giants, bolstered by a diet of foraged quinoa and self-awareness. There's been a smudging of the original format, so now emotional wellbeing is the curtain pole all the other factors hang off. They make shampoo from scratch in a trailer park. They half-tuck shirts. People say avocado a lot. I will say avocado again. As referees of everyday living, the Low Carb Malibu Kens are a living woke organism with very glossy hair. Goop come to life but less vagina-y. We live in times of competitive lifestyling, and the *Queer Eye* presenters are split atoms, dishing out poignant advice while orbiting their male protagonist nucleus. As always, there is attraction. There is repulsion. In just shy of forty-five minutes, the male subjects have breakthroughs.

As part of the constant reminder that gays have better taste, each atom has a speciality subject. Jonathan Van Ness is a unicorn raised in the forests of altruism, drinking from compassion rivers and nibbling on kindness moss. As the grooming atom, his magical strand of benevolence manifests in modernly masculine haircuts and home-made non-invasive skincare regimes. He's so emotionally lit, witty and caring I just can't imagine him functioning outside of the *Queer Eye* universe, because in the real world you have to navigate the awfulness of real people. Unlike the Spice Girls, there's a clear frontrunner of the five in the shape of Antoni, essentially because he's Canadian and not unattractive. He's a kind of catnip and Kryptonite for gay men, both repulsive and tempting. We loathe his beauty while also wanting to enter him. He's the foodie, but his *raison d'être* seems to be explaining avocados (them again) to rednecks and discouraging them from eating crisps. That's kind of it, but gays treat him like he threw the first avocado at Stonewall. On the back of these balsamic pearls of gastronomic wisdom Antoni has opened his own restaurant. Tan, the fashion one, recently discovered skinny-fit trousers and he won't shut up about them. Karamo does culture, meaning the men get theatre tickets and coffee-table books on Picasso. In a hideously asymmetric division of labour, Bobby is in charge of redesigning the subject's whole house from top to bottom, including defining areas for family and socialising, managing storage systems and the allocation of chores. Look closely and you'll see Bobby, dripping in paint, repositioning an interior wall while Antoni shucks a single avocado.

On the surface *Queer Eye* is pure entertainment, a five-way battle royale of one-liners and hot takes, and people saying fierce. But bubbly waters run deep. The presenters are an emergency response team for *toxic masculines*. You know the type: Middle American dads in MAGA hats, reared on pro wrestling and alligator wrestling and raw red meat and picklebacks. They love their wives but can only show it through working harder and hiding out in the den at the back of the house and very occasionally making physical contact with their kids. Gender reveals are the highlight of their emotional expression, getting wet-eyed as blue smoke escapes a popped balloon. These physically and emotionally sedentary men need a shake-up. Enter the five homosexual arbiters of taste and culture, as gayness floods the man-cave. They are four fingers and a thumb balled into a fist that smashes though lazy patriarchy and baggy cargo shorts. Where previous waves of gay culture focused on appearances, new *Queer Eye* is training the emotional muscles alongside the biceps. Getting happy is the new getting hot. As well as glossy hair, *Queer Eye*'s protagonist are conditioning the soul. Lather, rinse, repeat. Often the mind boggles at the lack of self-awareness and self-care the straight guy has. Honestly, is this man *really* learning to moisturise? Does he *really* drink redneck margaritas (tequila and Mountain Dew)? In each episode we're experiencing the complete rebuilding of a man from his soiled Timberlands upwards.

This holistic rejig peppered with feisty quips was the seismic shift Theresa May needed to reconnect not only with the public, but most of all *pregnant American TV pause* with herself. A spiritual makeover eradicating the oppressive accessories (chunky necklaces, Frida Khalo bracelets, Boris Johnson) that defined her tenure as prime minister. The woke elves would have set to work detoxifying the Conservatism: revamping her wardrobe, redecorating Number 10, and offering advice on grooming and lifestyle. Wellbeing would be key for Theresa, with a simple mantra guiding her transformation: less emotional baggage for a more emotional Brexit. At first it's baby steps – skipping through fields of wheatgrass – but we see a new May emerging: wearing French-tucked florals, calling the BBC 'well annoying', convincing a gang of yoofs to join her in banana-milkshaking Boris.

There's something about the gay experience that means you engage with your wellbeing and emotional state early on in life. You tend to have to question who you really are if you want to come out as a not-default male. Some people run toward their gayness, some run away. You can totally fuck it up and get suppressed, or go on all-night benders. Unhealthy decision-making is a rite of passage. After an

Advil and some emotional fracking, you eventually rationalise who you are to yourself. And with our velvet rage managed, we're able to see the world anew, understanding the power of an emotional enema. The fairy godfathers of *Queer Eye* use this formative format to help their chosen troglodyte evolve. It's not an emasculating encounter – the men actually get straighter. Or at least they get better at being straight. They take the time to look after themselves. They participate in the lives of their wives and kids. They listen. Each episode closes with a performative display of change: the former ugly duckling finally swanning out at an event, much like a girl in glasses in a teen movie ultimately going to prom in contact lenses and a decent dress. I imagine Theresa May in Ko Pha Ngan dressed as a Hare Krishna (Tory-blue robes), a shell necklace at her bosom. She's building a fire on the beach and recharging her crystals in the moonlight while nonchalantly squeezing on a jade vaginal egg. Making space to hear her husband. Making space to hear the country. Theresa. Definitely.

For me *Queer Eye* is an opening or fissure in straight culture where the light gets in, like plants leaning towards a window. It's a gay TV format but it speaks such common sense and entry-level, rudimentary self-care I'm certain it's not for gay men, because we're already somewhat woke. Our culture is actually being invaded like Poland. *Queer Eye* follows a familiar trajectory: ostensibly about gay men, and created for gay men, but commandeered by straight women (who then push it onto straight men). Women are its primary audience, and I guess they fantasise about magical fairies swooping in and reconditioning their menfolk. I can see the straight female attraction to the show. As a passive observer of straight relationships, I notice that it's never the man's responsibility to *get woke*. While men concentrate on leg day and stomp about making their bodies bigger, women seem to be doing most of the legwork when it comes to improving the texture of a relationship. Men just sort of show up when asked, and get praised for not wearing a suit.

For women, the only thing worse than not dressing your age is being a nag, and *Queer Eye* steps in as an aspirational operating system where inoffensive gay pixies do all the cajoling. Nag hags who make a man finally get his shit together. Lo! A man in chinos showing his emotions! Mainstream straight women binge the show and purge tears for their underwhelming husbands and boyfriends. If only the Fab Five could *Queer Eye* Steve. Begone, raffish beard. Begone, normally tucked shirt. The cast of *Queer Eye* are themselves well-adjusted dream husbands for straight women as they create dream husbands for straight women. Celebrities in their own right, they're chiselling away at their own bodies whilst sculpting datable straight men. Meta.

We've reached critical mass, and I've lost count of the number of times straight women have asked me if I'm watching *Queer Eye* or *RuPaul's Drag Race*. A girl in a pub once asked me, 'Why do gay men hate me?', and her use of gay men as an undifferentiated mass was its own answer. I then pretended to like her just to disprove her point. Some woman asked my mum, 'Who is the man and who is the woman?' about me and my husband, so I guess we have a little way to go. But these divs aside, shows like *Drag Race* are tokens of wokeness for the masses. Palatable sips of homosexual culture that can be tasted. Daytrips to acceptance. As elements of gay culture go mainstream they chip away at the cult energy that initially defined gayness. The displays of difference. The signalling of a diverted sexuality. Not diverted, exactly, just not *When Harry Met Sally*. And when Sally's dancing round her handbag at G-A-Y Late, it takes the edge off the surreptitious heritage that's passed down from years of illegal gayness behind closed doors. I have heard from older men that all the furtive gay sex lost its edge when it was decriminalised. Of course it's an inclusive scene, but sometimes I feel like a toddler who doesn't want to share his toys. I want to savour a bit of gayness for myself and my fellow gays. The parameters of gayness are like a sieve. Much like east London, or poppers, or anal sex, gays take the lead and straight women eventually follow, ultimately becoming the status quo. The eighties New York ballroom voguing is a historic example of the trickle-out-of-the-closet effect. *Sex and the City* was initially derided as middle-aged women acting like gay men.

I identify absolutely as a white middle-class woman and a basic straight guy, and a glistening gay man who needs to intervene. It's a big fish, little fish approach: huge important features, coupled with trivialities. Some of the traits are unchanging (I'm always black, I'm always gay), but others carry less weight (I eat avocados). They're passing fixations that I adopt and dote over like a stray cat, and drop just as swiftly. Food fads, workout whims and white socks, for example, are all part of an equation of the self that adds and subtracts fluidly. Some characteristics bury my gayness behind layers of internalised homophobia, and some celebrate it in rainbow colours.

With multifaceted queer spaces becoming abundant, I wonder what still *belongs* to gay men. The future belongs to the millennials who've reclaimed pink and cancelled gender. They're also doing anal, so I wonder what's really left for us tank-topped bum boys? Oddly, young people don't give two ticks about Madonna so we get to keep her, being provocative as ever but with relatively small reach on social. It used to be easy to know how to signal your gayness, but maybe we don't have to any more. Maybe acceptance and inclusivity eventually lead to indifference. That's a depressing thought. That's a comforting thought. Maybe indifference is the goal? True tolerance is gayness becoming meaningless because individuality isn't confined by where you stick your tongue. Gay culture has to be more than adjacent to straight culture. Gay culture has to be more than an Instagram filter that makes straight culture pinker. It has to be more than rimming and avocados. I don't know where we go from here.

Napkins and Serviettes

The emperor's new clothes taught us that nudity isn't kosher in the public forum. Clothes cover our erogenous zones to stop us from smashing in the street lest we see a nipple and pounce. Like eyebrows and pubes, clothes also serve to stop debris getting into our bits. There's nothing more irritating than a sandy crack. Pickpockets would have a tougher time if we were all naked because you could only really keep your spare change in your arse and that's harder to surreptitiously mine, but on the whole it's better to be covered up. Most people aren't hairy enough to go naked full-time without catching a chill.

The right coat says so much more than 'I want to be warm.' A Céline coat on the tube is a quiet statement of intent, the accented é of the Philo epoch is fashion treasure whether you can see it or not because the wearer is encased in history and knowing. Good clothes gold-plate our humdrum lives. People love to say style is timeless, as if fashion isn't a constant catalyst for mass consumerism, as if seeing a well-dressed person doesn't make you instantly want to buy better clothes. Dressing well isn't about clothes, really, it's about outfits. Ascending to the echelons of the well-dressed doesn't mean buying the right garments and wearing them when you go out, it's a product of thousands of micro-communications. The alchemy of a great outfit is more than fabric. It's a porridge of classics made modern, and heritage intertwined with visual proof you're not stuck in a rut. I love the idea of a capsule wardrobe: a battery of replaceable white T-shirts and perfectly tailored navy slacks. But I love to dress for the occasion too – pyjamas for the night train, shoes for when the yacht moors in Salcombe, shorts for visiting the Pyramids. I still covet out-of-my-price-range Burberry coats with fur collars and horsebit Gucci clogs. The only time it's OK to lie to your parents is when they ask what your clothes cost, because to splurge is to live. I'm somehow very happy to spend mountains of disposable cash on clothes that look like they've been grabbed from lost property at the end of a field rave. One madly expensive stretchy T-shirt still judges me back. On that note, Mel C is the fashion blueprint for most gay men because she's muscular and wears elasticated trousers that pull down quickly, and trainers that work for dancing all night.

Every time you glimpse a cat's arse or dogs humping in the park, remember that clothes differentiate us from the animals, regardless of trend. Covering up keeps human civilisation civilised. The wheels of society are greased by social codes, like the ones on swimming-pool posters. No shouting, no bombing, no heavy petting. Dig if you will the picture of you and I engaged in a kiss. You can't, because only teenagers snog on the street. More refined than an ASBO, most of these codes are about subtlety. The law says wear clothes, but we have individualised opinions on what constitutes *too much leg*. Private and public remain unhappy bedfellows. The sweetest taboo is anal (private), swiftly followed by not giving up your seat for an old person on the bus (public). The codes of a public forum are a psychological group chat we're all members of, an adhesive set of not-being-a-dick rules we all stick to. Everything we do in public is a subtweet, uttered under the breath, a metronome keeping us all invisibly moving to the same beat.

The idea of etiquette might be our most overly-evolved pursuit. Owning nice stuff and living a good life is one thing, but social etiquette is a hierarchy of signs, like the tiers of a wedding cake at the nuptials of two households, both alike in dignity. The cake is rich, and you don't want to accidentally stumble into the instant mousse at a shotgun wedding. Etiquette is an invisible semaphore of codes of conduct, pivoting on bizarre ideas like that you can have a fork in the wrong hand, or that saying *sweet* instead of *pudding* is unsavoury. It's not only about table manners, it's a system of polite behaviour that signals your social status: Carole Middleton had trouble infiltrating the royals because she used phrases like *pleased to meet you* and *pardon*, both of which sound to me like the height of politeness. First-Tinder-date-might-get-my-end-away-don't-ruin-it politeness. The word *pardon* is a notorious pet hate of the upper and upper-middle classes, making one appear ill-bred and even thuggish. The patron saint of etiquette, Nancy Mitford, described *pardon* as insufferably euphemistic.

Mitford makes me feel like Little Orphan Annie in Claridge's, or when the mermaid in *Splash!* bites the lobster. I am not well-groomed and I am not well-spoken. My pronunciation is abysmal, as nuanced as torching a crème brûlée with a can of Lynx and a lighter. I want to be sent on an etiquette course where they ladle a silver spoon into my mouth and transfuse my blood from red to blue. I will only consent to the most prestigious training – like accepting communion from the Pope, or singing lessons from Beyoncé – so preferably the programme is led in snowy Switzerland by a Nancy Mitford hologram who slaps the Lynx out of my hands. I will raise my social standing like Julia Roberts in *Pretty Woman* on Rodeo Drive (without the blonde wig and utility belt of condoms). Much like Viagra, I'd rather go hard or go home, so why stop at pronunciation? Modules that cover the people, places and things that should serve to overhaul my entire life. To infinity, and almond! It's like how I've always wanted to cook the perfect omelette, all gooey and rich and blasé. Firm and fragrant, with a sprinkling of herbs I didn't have to Google beforehand. The recipe is in my head, but it's more than a recipe, it's a deeper system of understanding flavours and temperatures and timings. From the outside I look like I'm just cooking, but inside I'm a bristling equilibrium of intuition and knowledge, all translating into casual flair. Butter? Oil? Cheese? No cheese? Always cheese? The end result is effortless. Classic and dependable. Simple components coming together in unity.

Each time I reach for the wrong fork the Mitford hologram smacks my hand with a cane, but like Dumbo's mother I'm slowly broken down to the ways of the master, and shrug off my dingy roots. After a natty montage – picture me reading Proust on the beach, getting into veal dishes, leotarding through a ballet class with a stack of books on my head, correctly pronouncing Timothée Chalamet, writing thank-you cards, learning all of 'Auld Lang Syne', picking up the right fork – I would be transformed to a state of pure refinement, like the sugar I used to eat in breakfast cereals before Nancy pivoted me to Génoise. The cold-turkey stage would be hard, weaning myself off *Project Runway* and Babybels, but they'd be succeeded by knowing *University Challenge* answers, Paul Thomas Anderson films and little jars of Fortnum & Mason cocktail onions.

The change in diet would be a shock to the system, but all refined persons eat oysters and caviar with the pearl spoon. Liberté. Égalité. Flatulence. Gout is the preserve of the rich. I'd then buy a house staffed with barely legal gay men. A stately homo. I'd wear butter-soft silk pyjamas in the daytime, while I laze on the chaise smoking a pipe and dextrously slicing a pear with a knife. I guess I'd still have a job, but it would be mysterious and would involve Greek shipping and numerous covert meetings, kind of like a modern-day Artful Dodger in velvet slippers. My life would reek of well-managed luxuries, like when you take a Coke from the hotel fridge and room service replace it while you're sightseeing. As the clock strikes Lucite, my IKEA furniture would morph into Vitra like Cinderella's pumpkin coach, and all my eBay ornaments would become impossibly sacred and scarce Lara Croft trinkets I picked up on my travels. Look at this stuff, isn't it neat, wouldn't you think my collection's complete? You'd be wrong. I would delete the Amazon app, eschewing the zero-hours-contract debacle for piles of musty books. Everything the genuine Magistretti lamplight touches would be a museum-quality reminder of my personal restoration and robust taste. My elaborate and painstaking method for sourcing rare rugs would make your toes curl, but I wouldn't make a big thing of it. All my candles would be full-price Cire Trudon columns in sophisticated colourways, and not the ones I currently have from the back of a pop-up in Bicester Village.

I would invent traditions that I'd stick to religiously, like picking up the cello on Sunday afternoons to serenade the family with a few familiar classical pieces designed to rouse a group. I would not bite my nails. I would not spill red wine. I would not do that laugh I do that sounds like a car revving and a donkey sneezing. There would be *petits fours*. And weekends on the Orient Express. Summers somewhere quaint in rural Greece (one of the islands that doesn't have an airport) with great seafood. I emerge from the programme as the transfigured Natalie Portman when she finally turns into the black swan, but less feathery and less fucking nuts.

In reality, truly posh people don't give a fuck about any of this stuff. OK, wait, they're horny for fascinators, the Chelsea Flower Show and that Jubilee flotilla. And like prehistoric man they learn to hunt, sail and ski before they start secondary school. They love kippers and speciality cheeses and roast game with *MasterChef*-level jus. They dress their kids either like Jacobean ghosts or minimalist architects – there is no in-between. And their cheaper amusements – Biros, tinsel, public transport – are mere distractions from the quenelles of quince and black cabs.

Their sense of etiquette underpins these pastimes, and is inherent to their breeding. They nurture it in their offspring so it becomes first nature. Like *The Lion King*, but it's the circle of upper-class life: Mufasa knows to say *napkin* instead of *serviette*, and doesn't so much pass this knowledge *down* to Simba but intuits it *into* him, like a BCG jab or a nicotine patch. When hatched in the battery farms of Chipping Norton, the crème de la crème of society have voodoo etiquette pins permanently thrust into them that stop them saying *greens* instead of *vegetables*. It's a complex system of myriad nuances, detectable in how people speak and interact and behave. For Turnip Toffs these modes of behaviour are ingrained from childbirth, with wetnurses muttering *Tally ho!* into the infants' ears and the toddlers cosplaying graduation from Oxford.

Oddly, it's not the elite who chase correct etiquette, it's the *hoi polloi* (another Mitford banned word. Using *hoi polloi* to describe plebs instantly identifies you as a pleb).

We, the plebs, are all trying to sound posh because we aren't. We're taking cues from the high-born, like the first time you go to the business lounge at T5 and wait to see how the person next to you builds their breakfast plate from the buffet. Upper-class modes of politeness trickle down through business class all the way back to economy. These distinctions of pronunciation and vocabulary – rhyming *forehead* with *horrid* – reveal wealthy aspirations. Any attempt at high-sounding language is a noticeable anomaly, like Del Boy in Waitrose. By overstating each phrase we common people show our hand. By spooning caviar onto our adjectives and wrapping every noun in mille-feuille, we're mimicking the rich like Eliza Doolittle in *My Fair Lady*: a parody of good breeding that the well-bred see straight through like a garish net curtain.

Posher shibboleths are pure aspiration, and people trying to ape them are garish social mountaineers, blaring foghorns of low breeding. Sounding wealthy is not an endeavour for the rich because they're already rich. You don't need to signal your affluence if you're genuinely loaded – that's a bit like pointing at your coat on the tube and shouting 'It's Céline!' This language system is knowingly understated, so it doesn't get tangled up in convoluted patter like a budget magician, or the vulgar frills of an overly decorated Christmas tree. High society is all about the concise and direct communication you only get on Grindr or episodes of *Supernanny*.

It's a question of taste, too. I once worked with someone with dreadful taste. At one point I was asked to stop describing things as 'naff' because I couldn't find the vocabulary to retort to certain ideas put on the table. Not a career high point, but the situation did highlight the subjectiveness of taste. Most bad taste is ironic, like a mullet or a piano-key tie, but the idea of having no taste is a conundrum, meaningless letters waiting to be puzzled out on *Countdown*. Like a flower leaning towards the sun I turned to Google and quickly discovered that taste is a made-up system of codes deliberately designed to stop people ascending socially. Taste, at its root, is about the ability to judge what is beautiful, good and proper, but upper-class taste is particularly characterised by refined and subtle distinctions. There are certain codes of taste – dresses, like children, can be too clingy – but the rich have time to fastidiously pursue their evolving brand of finery. When you don't have to earn a living, life can feel like great expanses of timeless void, like gays trying to entertain themselves between Madonna albums. Once you're getting the recommended eight hours' sleep a night and you've perfected your downward dog, the only thing left is sourcing shit nobody else can have with your near-clairvoyant intuition for the finer things.

Like charisma or a sense of humour, taste feels innate but it's built on foundations of understating. New money cannot scale the ranks of taste, regardless of what it can financially afford, because old money has ingrained historic values. New money is inherently vulgar because it's not forged in the flames of the elite. Even if she's totally rich because her dad invented toaster strudel and she can afford lunch at the Wolseley, she's still not in the club. Never in the club. We're slavishly shackled to our divisions, using invisible signifiers of taste to differentiate between people's social standing.

I can't shake the feeling we've over-evolved as a species. We've moved beyond societal functionality into etiquettical farce, judging each other for saying *toilet* instead of *lavatory*, or wearing Uggs unironically. We've shed our natural pelts and put clothes on, and now we think we're the dog's bollocks. But we're just animal instincts in people-shells, like a reverse Halloween where the monsters wear human costumes. Deep down we're still amoebas, but we have bitcoin. We're vaping raptors. Mere monkeys in Nikes. We're cavemen with smartphones. Homo sapiens on dating apps trying to attract other homos with hole pics, stalking like lions butt-first through the jungle of tops. Those clothes are coming back off.

Addendum: Hole pics have to be the end of civilisation, surely? If there's a higher power, she's bound to hit delete when she sees you pointing a camera down your own arsehole, cheeks splayed like a pinned butterfly in a frame. As a species, we don't really deserve to live beyond that, do we?

If the Prime Minister Smelled of Freshly Baked Bread

You can tell how hungover someone is by how loud they type. The stabbing of keys is a sure sign of an empty stomach and a thumping head. It's a countdown until they say 'I'm having pizza for lunch' and spend the afternoon staring into space. The FBI agent assigned to my laptop has seen me shotgun a French baguette like corn on the cob when I'm hungover trying to pay a utility bill. Me hungover is a nightmare because all I can concentrate on is supressing intrusive thoughts while the clock in my head counts down to the time I can go to bed without being rude. After a summer party I opened my emails at work and was so overwhelmed by the volume of material coming in I shut my computer down and went straight home. I ate a burrito on the bus.

Hangover foods often involve deep-fat frying, but all the best foods are beige, like the interior of an Upper West Side apartment. You don't need a hangover to enjoy crumpets, croissants or chips. Or pasties, or pies. Or waffles. Or numerous breads, the pale ones with the least fibre. Because carbs make everything better. Carbs are the optimistic *Live Laugh Love* teatowel of the food groups. It's impossible to bicker with a sandwich. Or argue with a steaming pile of mash. I've never met a sourdough I didn't like. The woman who put the cat in the bin wouldn't have done it if she'd had porridge for breakfast. Carbs curb violent tendencies. Want to strangle your boss? Have a rusk. Next time you're about to punch someone's lights out, have a rice cake. Tensions in the Houses of Parliament would be eased by the smell of deep-fried croquettes. It's hard to start a war over a plate of cheese straws. The future is a boiled egg and soldiers (withdrawing from Iraq). War is ovum if you want it. Give yeast a chance. We'd already have a Brexit deal if the prime minister smelled of freshly baked bread and acted more like the EU's rosy-cheeked baker, rather than some bad-haired bruiser in a cheap suit trying to sell you dodgy coke outside a provincial nightclub.

Speaking of star bakers. Have you seen those rugged ones at food markets in the Cotswolds? They always have ruddy cheeks and beards and giant floury hands. The kind of guy that has no idea he'd get shagged to death in London, legions of women clawing at his checked shirt and apron for a brief glimpse of his ciabatta. I always dream of retiring to the countryside and baking bread all day, but I think I'd be bored without my cosmopolitan elite bedfellows. I love a day trip to the farmhouse, but I need the pace of the city. Better to become slowly calcified by the London rat race and regularly scoff iced buns as a quick fix.

Like Magic FM, bread never fails to soothe. After food poisoning, when you have to unspice up your life, dry toast serves you like a royal aide, calming your stomach after a night on the throne. When you're tired and hollowed out from a week of undiluted angry emails, cheese rolls massage your back like John Travolta's masseurs. When you go out for dinner with your whole family and the waiter's been standing there for twelve mins while your sister reads out every single one of her dietary syns from a fitness app the bread basket pacifies. When life gives you lemons, flour makes a drizzle cake.

I've never done a full astrology birth chart, but I think my ruling planet is the potato, although anything that starts with a roux works too. Most humans need melty butter. And salty Jacobs crackers with soft Cheddar. And the sticky rice from my husband's Deliveroo even though I said I'm not eating rice so please don't order me any. Me eating my husband's food drives him mad. He hates to share dishes and has been known to order diversion sides that distract me from picking at his main dish. We always have to get two sides of fries lest I reach for his portion. He's OK about sharing mayo, that's how I know he loves me. The Ancient Greeks divided human physicality into four humours – blood, phlegm, the two biles – but I'd add mayonnaise to the list, an essential beige emulsion guaranteed to lube one socially and lift your temperament out of the gutter.

And if I ever split up with my husband I'll probably recouple with a roast potato. I was trying to think of a metaphor for being in love with roast potatoes, but modern love is just giving away most of your power. I would give away most of my power to a roast potato. I would probably do a 69 with a roast potato. I would go down on a roast potato in a temper. Carbs are pure comfort, and make you happy without the hassle of having to invest emotionally in another human, all beating heart and defecation. A roast potato doesn't leave the seat up. A roast potato doesn't fart. Who among us has never masturbated with a hot dog roll? Or fingered a Victoria sponge? Sex with cake is the sort of thing they do in hazing rituals in professional kitchens and nobody bats and eyelid.

I'd be the first to die in a space movie, but not because I'm black. The siren call of carbohydrate would be my unravelling. When the captain sends me to check on a strange noise in the cargo hold, I'd be more preoccupied with finding sachets of mashed potato to rehydrate than the alien with the drippy fangs right behind me. And then I'd be dead. I hope I get to taste starch one last time before I snuff it. I also hope they name a school after me, or better yet a weird plastic surgery procedure that makes you look like you've been awake all morning smashing through your to-do list. I couldn't really hack it in space with all the foods in gross plastic sleeves. Houston, we have a condom. Those vacuum slices of space pizza always look tragic, any last *joie de vivre* sucked out by a NASA vampire.

I once saw a documentary where the parents of an anorexic teenager found half a cheese toastie in her dressing-gown pocket. It was meant to be indicative of a young woman in the throes of a disease, but all I could think was *What a cheeky treat*. Imagine there's a cheese toastie in your pocket right now. Don't you feel exhilarated? A cheese toastie should come as standard in the pocket of every towel robe in every spa. When your bowels completely grind to a halt after a strict diet of apple-cider vinegar and silence, you find a lump in your pocket like Rose fingering the necklace in her trenchcoat as the *Carpathia* docks in New York. I would like all first responders armed with cheese toasties as standard. And all new cars fitted with a triangular toastie cavity next to the coffee cup holder. A toasite is the Esther Perel of gastronomy – soothing but transformative psychotherapy sandwiched between slices of wholegrain. Like a haunted house in a horror film, you're never alone with a toastie. A toothy grin of Red Leicester smiles back at you as you try on a Net-a-Porter dress you're definitely sending back. I like the sedimentary layers of cheese on toast, a kind of open-top toastie on a sightseeing tour. It's a stripped-back toastie, like the English Patient without his bandages. A thick layer of vintage Cheddar on a divan of grilled bread is a real indulgence. When people say eat the rich they sometimes mean Beyoncé, but usually they're referring to the super-posh Cheddar you get at general stores in hipster neighbourhoods. Welsh rarebit is cheese on toast after a couple of beers, a boozy comfort like your mum's breath when she picks you up from the babysit-ter's. Welsh rarebit is Kiehl's to cheese on toast's Imperial

Leather, but the classic toastie still offers the best reprieve from the grit of daily life.

Despite coordinated and sustained attacks from Dr Atkins, carbs have persisted. They have enduring, charming, universal appeal, like men before they get Me Tooed. Carbs are mathematical. Ever wondered what's the appropriate girth for an éclair? Or how many baps it takes to change a lightbulb? What's the recommended daily allowance of carbohydrate? I'm sure it's disappointingly small, like your arms after a year of lifting weights at Equinox. There was a story a while back with a scientist saying six fries was the recommended portion when you have a burger. Half a dozen fries … Like trying to power a Casio calculator with a thin slice of Duracell battery. The guy was obviously a lunatic, cackling at the stars and lobbing husks of pitta at the moon. Never in my life have I had one or two chips. Never in my life have I had a few bites of cake. Moderation isn't in my vocabulary. People who can have a bite of cake and not eat the whole thing are magical. Eating a couple of Pringles, popping and stopping at their leisure. For me, living your fullest life means committing to what's in front of you, not taking half of it home in a doggy bag for a rainy day. I'm eating the toastie in my pocket the second I find it. Imagine if McDonald's started doing six-chip servings of fries. People would riot. I would use the tiny batch of chips to make a pentagram on the counter and hex the whole building. I would burn it down like a women's libber's bra, igniting the trans fat and taking the golden arches down in flames in an explosion of chipped potato and McFlurry. I would throw myself under a horse to protest the minuscule servings. I would die as a sacrifice, so that you may get a proper fist of potato with your Happy Meal. Heaven, incidentally, is Dalí-esque, with surreal pastries warping over a barren yeasty landscape. *Hark!*, a chorus of melodic angels with crisps for halos are serenading me. Sing choirs of Pringles.

Never Let Me Go

Name the last time you used your body without intention. You moved and you weren't trying to achieve something. If I mention how you're breathing right now you automatically engage with it. You breathe deeper for more oxygen, or shallower to prove me wrong. Everything we do physically has some kind of objective, big or small. You walk-run to make the next tube. You do Pilates for core strength. You kickbox to get your heart rate up or your hips smaller. You do crunches to be more attractive and you squat for thigh cleavage. You dance on that pole for the Benjamins. Movement is always in pursuit of something.

I'm massively oversimplifying, but the intention of yoga is to clear out your constipated mind like wellness laxative. A spiritual colonic. All your organs getting finger-banged by moving meditation into a transcendent euphoria. Yoga is WD40 for your bones. Yoga unblocks your u-bent brain. Yoga grafts spirituality onto your soul like an oblong of soft skin from your thigh. The teachers say you can spend the whole class lying down, but it's difficult to stick your head in the sand and ostrich for a full sixty minuets. As some point you step, hop or float to the top of your mat (this is a little yoga joke). Downward dogging doesn't solve problems, but gives you the headspace to tackle them like Pelé (this is a little football joke).

Physically, you get more flexible, which we all know means bendy in bed, your happy baby pose making way for a happy adult. You get toned, which means thin enough for your tightest clothes. Your sleep is deeper for longer, like an M&S meal, and you snooze through that alcoholic alarm that usually wakes you up with a jolt as you withdraw from Breezers. I come to yoga to ensure a certain equilibrium in my body, balancing my sedentary lifestyle with movement, lest people think I've let myself go. Letting yourself go is the rock bottom of a successful life, because it implies a certain idle laziness and an inability to hold onto anything that matters. The idea of letting oneself go is abhorrent, and a form of social control I willingly subscribe to like a culture podcast. Letting go is toxicity in a seemingly charmed life. The dated notion that we must monitor our inputs and outputs at all times is somehow still with us. Never let me(self) go. I can think of maybe forty times I've let my body down this week alone. How do I aggress thee? Let me count the ways. I ate triangle after triangle of Laughing Cow (more than six). I have this glorious habit of letting butter melt into my toast and then adding a second round of butter that stays fairly solid, almost like a slice of cheese. I went over thirty-eight hours without a shower. Sometimes before yoga I just wet-wipe the top five dirty places on my body (it's vital to do this in the right order). Sometimes I don't fully undress to masturbate. I don't spend an evening in the bath with a scented candle connecting with my senses and then pleasuring myself. I just knock it out and get on with my day. I still wear my favourite white T-shirt with a chocolate-ice-cream stain on the front even though the stain is visible from space. When people mention the stain I act surprised and disappointed, as if I'm seeing it for the first time and my T-shirt's ruined and I can't wear it again. I always wear it again. Before getting into bed with my husband I squeeze my spots and blob them in Germolene, quite a bit of it round the mouth. I'm significantly less kissable but my skin is better in the mornings. I take my phone to the sit-down toilet nearly every time.

But I still, despite my better judgement and all-round wokeness, notice other people letting themselves go. The let-gone aren't lazy exactly, they're just not self-optimising. Letting yourself go is succumbing to the passing of time, rather than freezing yourself at your peak and holding on for dear life. Reaching the summit of yourself takes massive persona-extension and then tireless energy not to let your natural elasticity snap back. The let-gone have lost their grip on all the romanticised trappings of youth, the illusion of vitality. It's not a sad existence, it's just not trying to move into the future still looking like they did in the past. They've let go of impossible aspirations, and unreasonable goals, and putting inordinate amounts of pressure on themselves to constantly grow. They accept their lot in life. They have settled. They *are* settled. Marrying spouses who don't tick enough of the right boxes. Doing jobs that don't 360 satisfy. Sharing beds with their pets. Letting their kids eat sugary cereal. Repeating holidays to the same place, never saying 'Wouldn't it be nice to go Mumbai for New Year's?' They have brief sex without the rigmarole of hypersexualised outfits or foreplay or adequate dilation. They watch Saturday-night TV rather than their figures. They wear comfortable clothes. They have hand-me-down garden furniture, but not in a cool way. The let-gone host coffee mornings where nobody wears make-up and everybody says yes to Battenberg.

The least let-gone months of my life happened a few years ago when I took a concoction of Goop vitamins called Balls in the Air. I remember the ninety-day subscription with a sepia-tinted, misty-eyed, tightly-held reverence. After I downed six capsules my balls flew up and stayed up, juggled like no other period in my life. My concentration was razor-sharp, my days were focused and my social calendar was popping, strutting though Soho with a *Tell me I'm pretty, cowards!* look on my face. The ingredients were mainly vitamin B12 and fish oil, but I've never felt more upbeat. What a time to be alive. They were a little moreish, and I gobbled some of my boss's too, and that's how an addiction starts. I was on a roll, and I didn't care. She asked if I was stealing them and I denied it. Addicts lie. But I was hooked on the uppers. The source ran dry and I tried to replicate it with Boots cod liver oil and a good multivitamin, but that's like going from intravenous heroin to sniffing a Pritt Stick. It's an expensive luxury to import vitamin supplements from the States, so I didn't. I will forever chase the dragon of Goop Balls in the Air.

Speaking of moreish, I'm groggy because I love over-the-counter sleeping liqueurs, and I need them for the requisite eight hours sleep a night. Sleep is a key factor in looking like you have your shit together. People saying you look tired when you're not tired is a prestige micro-aggression masked as concern. Don't be fooled. They mean you look like you've let yourself go. With sleeping draughts, I started out quite medieval and witchy, like the aggressive woman with the cataracts from *Robin Hood: Prince of Thieves*. Mugwort spleen in fennel tea or whatever. I was intrigued by administration, potency and efficiency. As with most things in my life, I've streamlined the process and usually down a capful of Night Nurse when sleep evades me. Which is most nights. I ran out of my most magic beans, Advil PM, six months ago, and can't get anyone to mule it back from the US. They're actually a bit too much, too moreish. A swig of Night Nurse tips you from tired to asleep without the nagging existential mind chatter. My mind is quiet as an adult library where people still respect each other. The worst thing is pretending to be ill when stocking up. Any pharmacist worth their salt will repeatedly ask you how sick you are, and you can't break character for a second.

Kids are essentially back-ups for letting yourself go, because they might become independently wealthy and get you into a nursing home in Florida long after your ability to earn collapses. Not only did I learn the fierce power of piano music and vocals when I watched Doris Day saving her kid's life with a rendition of 'Que Sera Sera' in a Hitchcock film, but it also clicked for me that children have extraordinary utilitarian value outside of fetching your tea and eventually inheriting your wealth. People cite *happiness* and *personal fulfilment*, but the main reason to have kids is to teach them to play the piano. A few years in and you can recreate Marie's Crisis in your front room. Nobody in the history of the planet has ever said 'They sing round the piano, they've really let themselves go, lazy fucks.' Once your offspring are fully trained you'll spend Christmas Eves gathered around the baby grand in matching waistcoats glugging Bailey's and singing showtunes. If that's not Christmassy, I don't know what is.

I will strive to achieve the level of importance and self-care of the man next to me on the mat with a yoga towel and a separate face towel and a reusable bottle who remembered to get a sponge block before the class. It's easier to think I'm nailing my core strength when I'm comparing myself to a short woman in an old T-shirt who looks brand new to the practice. I always work really hard when there are more men at yoga. I'm not really a dick swinger by nature, but something quietly competitive sneaks out when men appear on nearby mats, and I promise to quit salad dressing forever and become *American Psycho* fit. Patrick Bateman wasn't happy exactly, but he never took his eye off the ball, and he got laid a bunch.

Never letting yourself go means committing to your body at twenty-one and arresting any further development, which I've heard is especially difficult after you've had a baby. There are all sorts of bogus diets to attempt aesthetic recovery, but if all else fails fall back on your personality. Is it worth mentioning that inner beauty is not really what our multi-billion-dollar capitalist society is all about? Alicia Keys has that covered, I think.

Regardless of your natal status, being an Adonis takes real work. Long hours running on the spot and lifting on the spot and punching on the spot. I'm obsessed with a friend of mine who whacks a concrete Terrys chocolate orange into the ground like he's digging for oil. Once at hot yoga there was an American woman who looked reasonably lithe, but she was wearing a full tracksuit and a hoodie. A tracksuit and hoodie is the maddest thing to wear at hot yoga, like wearing a foil blanket over a sweatshirt over a thermal vest at the beach. She huffed loads and swore under her breath in American, but the most shocking thing about her was when she took off her hoodie and there was another hoodie underneath. Imagine how hot she was – like Jessica Rabbit sucking off a blowtorch. Maybe she was a jockey trying to shed waterweight ahead of the Grand National. A vision of her smouldering hot life has stayed with me henceforth.

The unwritten rule of yoga is to be in the moment and not judge other people, but the second-hoodie woman is worth a mention for her sheer commitment to never letting herself go. I find Americans, in general, a touch too upbeat. Their likeability is always dialled up to eleven. When I lived in New York on a tourist visa for ninety days I started to believe I was amazing because people kept telling me I was amazing. I'm averse to American clichés, but they're like Coldplay albums: I hate this song but holy fucking shit why is my fucking foot tapping? My tourist tenure was in 2006, so I became a monstrous Myspace psycho, living in a Brooklyn loft, with a taste for compliments. Americans have this Cheeto-fuelled enthusiasm that doesn't tally with the nuanced British way of being a miserable fucker while eating Eccles cakes. Sarcasm isn't even a thing in America. Do you ever feel like a plastic bag? Not to worry. If you look shit, Americans tell you you look great. If you're sad they give you mood-enhancing pills. If you kill someone, they pass you another gun. The American Dream is exactly that, a fantasy of thoughtless platitudinal response without a moment's pause for reality. I know I sound like I don't like Americans, but it's not that. It's their apple-pie niceness that leaves me disconnected. Any Americans I've met who can see the falsity of their own platitude culture are all either super-depressed or functioning workaholics. I'm almost jingoistic about being British, and that's bad, because we've Brexited ourselves and ruined everything. OK, thinking this whole thing over, both sides of the Atlantic are doomed.

Not letting yourself go as a British person means pretending you're not putting any work in. Like tap dancers not grimacing on stage as their legs seize up like jerky. The work has to be covert and nonchalant. You're a natural beauty with inherited ruddy cheeks and your own teeth. For that reason I think of my wrinkles and grey hairs as distinguishing. I will not become one of those Just For Men men with a full head of abnormally dark curls. I don't want to be like Simon Cowell with happy teeth and sad eyes and an inappropriately deep V-neck that reveals a Dairylea triangle of mahogany flesh. I want to look like I haven't made an effort while making numerous concealed ones that invisibly strain my adrenal glands. I'm grappling, as we're all hastening to do, with the dichotomy of how things look vs how things feel. As I get older I'll look like a well-loved, scuffed table – perfectly imperfect. I'm just going to get these forehead wrinkles threaded and then I'll age gracefully.

Kevin Costner Drinks His Own Piss

Not sure if you've noticed, but the planet is dying. Michael Jackson told us to heal the world: a hymn for the planet we didn't listen to because we were watching him moonwalk. There are people dying, if you care enough for the living. Whatever our distraction, climate change is now upon us. It snuck in the back door and now it won't leave the house party, killing the vibe with shit music, drinking the last of the cold beer and puking up into all the plant pots. Is it too late now to say sorry? The short answer is yes. The longer, denser, more scientifically researched and accurate answer is yeeeeeeeeeees. It's too late to refreeze the ice caps, so Jack Dawson's thawing corpse is floating up from the bottom of the ocean, preserved and intact like a Linda McCartney bean burger at the back of the freezer. We can't remove the carbon dioxide from the air the same way we can't suck a flu jab out of your veins as you turn autistic. It's too late for a sticky label pasted over 50 per cent of the oceans like the warning on a cigarette packet.

Mother nature is a teat we've collectively sucked dry, leaving shrivelled milkless breasts for our descendants. The adults of tomorrow will receive planet earth from us like passing on herpes. I don't want to be a climate bore, but my grandkids are going to live underwater, and not in a sexy merman way. The globe is sullied like Monica Lewinsky's dress, dry clean only but we've drenched it in detergent. The once tepid bath of the sea is starting to simmer, about to boil over. We're living in the hothouse at Kew Gardens, a wet T-shirt competition that everyone loses. We're fully clothed in the sauna but we're locked in like an episode of *Columbo*, smearing the murderer's name on the steamy glass. We've entered into asymmetric warfare with mother earth and she doesn't stand a chance against our relentless desire for red meat and new jeans and vanilla spiced lattes. But most of us are still waiting for biblical floods before we stop buying yoghurt or separate out our plastics.

We watch as teenagers have climate angergasms on the street, recycled placards held aloft, and like the images of them sailing across the Atlantic to highlight climate meltdown. We're concerned, but not *that* concerned. Concerned enough to buy a KeepCup, sure, but not enough to change our behaviours. We can be sad about cyclones, landslides, floods, droughts, but we need an extinction-level event like in the movies before we start working on being less avoidant with our toxic lifestyles. Our aspiration for more stuff and more convenience stays belligerently intact. We treat the planet like a nice bit on the side after a mediocre first date.

We're not bothered, we're not committed. The planet's fucked and we're all still planning nice summers and Christmases and birthday mini-breaks and date nights. We're still bucket listing. Self-improvement outweighs planetary implosion, striving to be our best selves while overlooking the greenhouse gases creeping under the door. Enjoying the blistering sun in March. Spraying aerosols under our arms. A suicide cult committed to fingering the hole in the ozone layer before we completely fuck it. The rainforest is important, but so is the question of low-rise jeans actually 'coming back'. We've had too many joyrides in daddy's Jaguar (diesel) and those Balenciagas, the ones that look like socks (the litres of water needed for a spool of cotton are their own Stacey Dooley documentary). We're wolfing down methane-producing beefburgers as the equator gets so hot it evaporates into a gas and dissipates into outer space. We're the coastal elite, screwing in energy-saving lightbulbs as the rising ocean laps at our ankles. Still calling an Uber when the tube would keep things more stable. Still jetting to the Alps to ski every February (actually, skiing will be a key skill for nuclear winter). Sucking on that content teat as ecosystems collapse. Laughing at memes as the bees disappear at an alarming rate. 'Accidentally' still eating almonds. 'Accidentally' still eating avocados.

The signs of ecological collapse have been there for decades. Red flags everywhere, like holes on a golf course or the candles on your nan's birthday cake. Acid rain on your wedding day. Sun is shining, the weather is sleet. The only upside to climate meltdown is that we won't have to worry about seasons and seasonal dressing. I'm secretly looking forward to the eternal sunshine of the eternal sunshine, though we're not certain on which way things will tip. We might get infinite sleet. Constant drizzle feels marginally more manageable but not altogether exciting. I love skiing so an enduring chalet climate would work as long as there's fondue. Come to my summer BBQ, the dress code is hazmat. This June's gonna punish you. If not climate-change deniers, we're a generation of climate-change deferrers, putting off drastic action for a few years while we leave carbon footprints across the globe on Ryanair flights in leather shoes. We're preoccupied with group chats and DMs as the stars sputter out above our heads. We're Eurostar apologists. Allies of the floating island of plastic. Loudly giving up straws as lip-service to the ocean but not quitting fish. Never fish. Fish are full of omega-3. We spiral downwards towards our inevitable annihilation, like the toys approaching the furnace in *Toy Story 3*, but we're still concerned with anti-ageing treatments. We fill the sea with microbeads. Our complexions brighten and dark skies draw in.

If Hollywood is to be believed, the apocalypse is overdue. Some wrecker of civilisation will win out. A cleanse, a purge, a plague of locusts. Zombies maybe, or dinosaurs, or King Kong. The end of the world will be an absolute scene, like those bone-crunching stampedes on Black Friday. The extinction-level event that wipes some (most) of humanity out like hot water on ants is imminent. I for one feel fairly prepared. Nothing says I'm ready for the apocalypse like a six-pack of sparkling San Pellegrino in the fridge. I have about forty cans of tinned cherry tomatoes and Lavazza in my larder, so our vitamin-C and caffeine levels will stay consistent as we wait to die. And if the wireless goes down I have a podcast-length voicemail from my mum to listen to in full. Whatever finally kills us off – the rising tides of the melting ice caps, cow farts, the deep impact of an asteroid – some brawny and noble individuals will survive. Jake Gyllenhaal, maybe, or one of the Hollywood Chrises. Kevin Costner has a good track record. And like a cockroach, Gordon Ramsay will survive out of sheer bloody-mindedness. Kim Kardashian makes it, bolstered against the storm in a cocoon of her own sexiness, using her implants as an internal flotation device. Donna Air makes it because she is the Groundhog Day of second chances, transcending *Byker Grove* to become a royal. An actual royal. Air is a survivor, moulded from Geordie grit and determination. Ditto Michelle from Destiny's Child. These celebrities will come together as deities to forge the new world after the tidal wave recedes and the fires go out. But as the tectonic plates realign and the magma cools, I couldn't help but wonder … what's my skillset twenty-eight days later? What indispensable qualities do I bring to the rebuilding of civilisation? How handy am I on New Earth? After all these years on the planet, what skills have I accumulated?

The aftermath of the apocalypse probably doesn't need creative direction, and my skillset outside of that is somewhat niche and not altogether transferable. I stopped reading the *Daily Mail* about five years ago. Is that a skill? The closest I've come to survival mode is to reinstall the Ocado app on my phone. I could probably jump into a swimming pool in my pyjamas like I saw on *Blue Peter*. I could probably make a papier-mâché Tracy Island from a cornflakes box too. I could probably upcycle a chair. Well, paint it. Well, if somebody brought me the paint and the brushes and there wasn't too much of a focus on fussy little things like finish. Oddly, I've learned little to no survival skills from buying Adidas trousers off Sports Direct. The FBI agent assigned to my IP address just watches me in my pyjamas Googling 'winter sun' and eating tacos. Someone once hacked my phone like Milly Dowler's, but it was too boring to expose in a national paper because it was just the near-silent sound of my thumb scrolling as I read my own tweets.

Nobody actually needs another fashionable coat or Birkin, but even Anna Wintour knows how to sew Alaïa handbags into a tent. We all know the producers give Bear Grylls cans of Coke and Twixes between takes, but at least he has some genuine survival knowledge. Who among us can say they could withstand the sub-zero temperature of an icy river with a Jonas Brother? Certainly not me. I'll emerge on New Earth with filmic references to homosexual love and social injustice. *Thee Billboards Outside Ebbing, Missouri* taught me feelings, but not practical steps to hunt and gather. Live-tweeting, huddled under a blanket at Somerset House drinking rosé and identifying with both Elio and Oliver in *Call Me By Your Name* felt important at the time, but now feels somewhat indulgent. Speaking of Kevin Costner and his back catalogue, I learned a little about forest foraging from *Robin Hood: Prince of Thieves*, but Christian Slater's historically inaccurate hair was a distraction. Costner's *Waterworld* was apocalyptic, but much more about warring water goths than handy survival tips. I only really remember him drinking his own piss, which I'm not mad about, to be honest. I learned pop-star protection from *The Bodyguard*, but zilch about insulating mud huts or capturing solar energy. Outside of the dance numbers, the most haunting scene in that film was them saucily cutting a single hair in half. I could definitely saucily cut a single hair in half while the first responders first respond.

My survivalist CV is short because my skills are more stylised domesticated habits than exact talents. I make a mean cup of coffee in my Alessi stovetop coffee-maker. Even the worst people learned how to make a fire at Scouts or Brownies or whatever. I went to Woodcraft Folk, but I don't remember any wooden crafts. I remember doing an impromptu play about *racism in the playground*, but I'm not sure how that will square with the furtherance of a planet in crisis mode. I can rustle up a dinner from a corner shop armed only with a fiver and a sense of imagination, but will there be any corner shops left? I don't lack confidence – my confidence never gets dented. It's like a natural shield. It remains malleable but protective, like the jelly in a pork pie, absorbing any tremors between real life and my meaty self. Confidence is a life skill, but not a *survival* skill. People will need doctors, but doctors needn't be confident. A shy doctor can still splint a leg. A shy archer can still catch dinner. A shy lover can still procreate.

What else is there? Despite all the noise I make I'm a great listener. I'm aware that when you're in Pompeii on volcano day, suffocating on ash at the beach, a great listener isn't your first port of call. I can't drive, but I once had a very short archery lesson and here I am still talking about it. I'd love to try falconry like in *Kes*, or training homing pigeons like in *Geordie Racer*. Oh, wait, I had a guided tour of an organic garden in Umbria, and later ate the harvested greens at dinner, so I could be the guy that oversees any foraging. I'm adaptable, but by that I mean I don't get in a strop about missing the trailers at the cinema any more, or fly off the handle when my orange juice gets left out of the fridge. (That particular peccadillo earned me the nickname Stropicana for a few months in my twenties.) I also compulsively mention the fact that I've never been to LA. Not sure where that fits in, but I'm sure it's a plus somehow. When I get dressed, I'm not afraid to clash patterns or bright colours, so maybe I could be a human flare. Clashing prints is like that dazzle camouflage on that boat in Hydra. I could dress like the boat in Hydra. I'm also very good at hydrating, which will of course a be a major issue after the extinction-level event. People will need water, though I have zero skills at finding it. I guess my role could be reminding everyone to hydrate regularly after a clean water source is found. That's my survivor niche. A water alarm. A hydration nag wearing double checks. Am I grasping at straws here? To be honest, after the apocalypse I'll be a dead weight. Like a problematic university mate, I'm the person you should leave behind. The tide was high and I held on, but after doomsday I'll just be sitting around in three types of stripe trying not to die.

The most annoying thing about this dystopian future is that annoying people will prosper. As the couch potatoes and Instagram influencers die from malnutrition and lack of attention, the virtue-signallers will inherit the earth. You know the ones. The organic eaters. The finger knitters. The pretentious foragers. People who don't spend their time putting together pattern-clash outfits. People who are interacting with the natural world on a primeval level. That's who gets the planet. The virtuous – in their sturdy shoes and cream work jackets and Fräulein Maria dresses the poor didn't want – are already one step ahead of the apocalypse. I used to think of them as the truly bored. It's like some people are so flat they have to add a raising agent, like bicarbonate of soda. 'Imagine being so boring you have to make your own cup,' I would say. This back-to-basics approach to every aspect of your life is one of many middle-class pursuits. Deliberate analogue living to create a simpler, less technological way of being. Like milling your own flour. Baking your own bread. Icing your own cakes. At the extreme end, some of them forge swords and shields and re-enact historic battles. If you can afford all the stuff you actually need to survive – housing, medicine, a 4-bed in a good catchment area – you then have the luxury to adopt a sort of humble self-sufficiency. Middle-class pursuits crave a return to the basics, a reconnection to the planet and its peoples and salt pigs and eighteenth-century ramen bowls. *The Good Life*. Eggs from the chickens in the garden and potatoes from the soil. Outsource good wine because any wine made locally to London is a vinegar gag. Let's churn our own butter.

Somewhere along the way, ceramics stopped being about making pots and started being about the signalling of making pots. Not so much clay on a pedestal but a whole lifestyle that spins around and showcases a certain type of 360-degree worthiness. I get the appeal of making something with your hands, it's beautiful and human and sublime, but ceramics have been co-opted by divs. Basic people who work in the media trying to signal an expression of how in touch with their creativity they are. Grayson Perry was a catalyst. And a legend. But ceramics dropped over a cliff. They became very hen-do. And who wants a ceramic dick when the furtherance of the planet is at stake?

The ceramicists get the last laugh. They're readying themselves for the biblical flood, a quiet army of cavemen and stonemen and ironmen. Living off the earth, kneading unleavened flatbreads and whipping up little green salads from nearby allotments. At one with nature like people who swim at Hampstead Ponds outside of heatwaves and bank holidays. After the flash floods, the annoying potters on Instagram create vessels to carry water. So much more handy than cutting a single hair in half. Within a month they'll have fully carpeted two-storey homes. They'll organise a decorous line at the food bank they've set up to help the less fortunate survivors. There will be no fighting. There will be no looting. There will just be the rolling champagne socialism of the elite.

I could try and get used to the utopia that emerges after the world ends. A phoenix from the flames that reminds everyone to hydrate properly. I could do medieval living in a modern way, which sounds quite steampunk. The silver lining of the apocalypse is all the steampunk people dying out and their clockwork paraphernalia smelted by molten lava. Maybe all the judgemental arseholes on Mumsnet don't make it either, engulfed in disapproval and criticism. Everyone hotter than me at my gym dies too, but that's only fair. And all the cruellest teachers at my secondary school get tied together like a king rat, eventually gnawing off each others' limbs. Ten per cent of the people who describe themselves as 'bubbly' survive, because God is merciful.

In our slimlined society I'd flourish. I'd dial down the dazzle-camo clothing. I've never worn a chainmail vest, but part of me thinks I'd suit a chainmail vest. I could swap out Campari spritzes for homebrew mead. I'd be happy to use wonky pots instead of my Conran plates. If nearly everyone is dead, I wonder who'd stop me living in the Acropolis? Or running round Paris Hilton's house in the dead of night like the Bling Ring? Or bathing in the Princess Diana memorial fountain? Or touching all the art at the Met? Or wanking over Captain von Trapp? Or wearing Leonardo DiCaprio's heart shirt from *Romeo + Juliet*? Or neatly striking out Donna Tartt's name in copies of *The Secret History* and writing my own in? Maybe I'll find the warehouse of Fortnum's Christmas hampers and eat the tube of shortbread from each one. Maybe I'll start smoking again because why the fuck not? Maybe the dazzle clothing will creep back in. I'll be lonely, but eating prawn cocktail Walkers in Tutankhamun's death mask will ease the pain somewhat. Armageddon is suddenly sounding extremely manageable.

The Affair

I'm so in love with my phone it's like I'm having a secret affair with it behind my husband's back. Or right under his nose. The phone and I meet at The Lobster Roll in the Hamptons, with my great lips and animal magnetism. All covert text messages and clandestine afternoon clinches. I've been seeing my phone for a while, but I still get the rush of excitement. Electricity. An intimate, emotional, visceral connection. When I'm with you all I get is wild thoughts. It's a flame that doesn't dim, a fling that doesn't dampen. A rush of blood to the head without the need for ibuprofen. A tryst of constant liaisons. Flirty messages. Mischievous pictures. Illicit typing. It's moreish, too, the thrill of the vibrating notification in my pocket. I can feel its pulse against my leg. I slip away to the bathroom to privately check my updates. The gratification is instant: I am understood, I am loved, I am adored. But it's not really the phone I'm having an affair with every time I pick it up. It's not notifications or apps I'm falling deeper in love with – it's myself.

I know how that sounds.

As sentient beings who've watched *Quantum Leap* we recognise that we can't be in two places at once. It's scientifically impossible to inhabit more than one space at any one time, but my phone warps the dimensions. I can simultaneously be on Tumblr and Twitter and Tinder and Tidal. My attention diffused like a Lush bath bomb, diluted like cheap plonk. My consciousness is a single serve of hotel-buffet butter, but spread across four slices of toast. A very thin whisper of jam diffused across the portions until you can barely see it and you can't taste it at all. A weak hue of red from a rogue sock in the wash. It's a reciprocal relationship where the quality plummets. Through our phones and their connectivity we convince ourselves we're getting closer, but there's a shallowness across a wider audience, like spilling your sangria across the deck of a booze cruise. There's a chasm between the real you and all the platforms you're micromanaging. You don't make an impact. You don't touch the sides. You're a chipolata thrown down Regent Street.

When I'm with my husband I'm always with my phone, and it fills the space around us, demanding my attention in a way I would never let another human being encroach on our time. Take a typical weeknight. Dishing out likes as I sit on the bed in a towel is no biggie. I arrive on time to meet my husband, but I'm simultaneously WhatsApping my mum about her dinner in Florence and recommending a restaurant. Through the cinema trailers I'm watching my mate's blood sugar crash as she cuts out refined sugar. The notifications don't stop, so in a way I'm never completely on the date, because my phone is interrupting like a Tamagotchi that needs feeding. The phone trespasses on our time together, but quietly, stealthily, like a cat burglar stealing intimacy rather than jewellery. It's not even work emergencies that zap me out of the moment. It's endless chatter with a few genuine rofls. Celebrity Instagrams. Screengrabs of celebrity Instagrams. Adult women in jelly shoes and socks. LA vampire women drinking green juice. New York tourists near pepperoni pizzas. People going nuts over ramen. Kardashians in neon. The Olsens, dressed as Dementors, smoking outside their office. Hypebeasts in baggies. Millennials in millennial pink eating avocado in millennial-crop trousers. Nineties blondes. Gay men in bathrooms. Gay men on beaches. Gay men in big groups of gay men, all inexplicably topless. Chats with gay men about their skincare regimes. A meme of an Oscar speech coupled with a quip about seasonal depression. Lucian Freud paintings. Alexander Calder mobiles. David Hockney pools. Horny likes for hot people. Pity likes for lonely people. Restaurants with branded plates. That Paris potato with the caviar. A meaningless scroll of mass-aesthetics. None of this is important.

Conveniently, neither my husband nor I particularly mind. The phones on silent between us were normalised in rapid time. There was a period about five years ago when we'd call each other out on it with a stern 'Babe …' and wait for the other person to slide the device away like fallen flakes of cheese straw. I was indignant at the suggestion that I was too involved with my phone, but then, by some alchemy, we just became complacent about their constant presence. Now we both allow it. I chat. He chats. We sometimes talk to each other about the chats we're having. I rarely ask him to come off his phone. He's more likely to dish out a stern 'Babe ...' if I post something with too much flesh or where you can see his teenage tattoo.

Let me ruminate for a second about the two guys I'm seeing. Is my phone better than my husband? Do I need a husband if I've got a phone? I'm committed to the one-note anxiety oblong in my hand, and also to the incredibly nuanced ever-changing flesh oblong in my bed. But can my phone offer the same relationship perks? Does my phone fart in bed? No, and I can turn my phone off when it's acting up, which is ten points to Gryffindor. A phone doesn't need reminding to book flights. A phone doesn't leave his crap everywhere. A phone would never ask if we could have some meals without cheese. Ouch. I do this amazing feta scramble thing, which I thought everybody loved. A phone would never ask me to stop making the feta scramble thing. (Incidentally, Cheddar scramble sounds like orienteering in the drizzling rain, a kind of corporate night-mare team-building exercise.) A phone doesn't say 'I'm a bit too *young* to remember that, darling.' A phone can delete bad memories, and erase evidence of bad behaviour, which is a godsend.

But a phone doesn't notice when you need a hug. A phone doesn't stroke the cat for me when I'm abroad and homesick. A phone doesn't buy me McDonald's nuggets, nor ask me to transfer the money. A phone shows me exactly what I look like in intimate detail, rather than telling me I look great. A phone doesn't pretend my hairline is the same as it was in my twenties. A phone doesn't dance with me in the kitchen when it gets back from work (usually something euphoric, rather than a slow dance). A phone won't scrape me off the floor at Chiltern Firehouse on a Tuesday and pay my martini-laden tab and tell everyone it's time to call it a night. My husband's never done that either; I just thought it was getting too lovey-dovey, and a party animal anecdote felt restorative.

It's a draw on how much I miss them when they're not with me. Baby when you're gone I realise I'm in love. But I guess that's the fun of men. Their presence. Their variety. Their inconsistency. A phone is predictable, and despite the notifications and reminders, the truth is it's just not that into you. My phone has a façade of constant attention. And my husband's attention to me is imperfect and transient, because constant attention is a crazy way to operate after ten minutes, let alone ten years. My husband's attention wasn't designed in Silicon Valley to give me a dopamine hit and keep me engaged. His attention is genuine and flawed and I have to work for it, like all the best things.

As a side note, I hope you can see the relationship like I see it. Not a dreamy painting, not a gritty photograph, more of an ongoing fluctuation. A rolling agreement to be better to each other and for each other. An endeavour, an attempt, a pursuit. Getting married is the weirdest thing, because you make a public commitment out loud about foreverness, and it's too big to fathom. You can't get your head around forever. It's too fucking long. Like *X Factor* contestants, we've made the song our own. We've agreed to work on what comes next as a team. We'll manage the small and large things together. That's our marriage. Not a relief that I found *The One*. Not an excuse to coast. Not a sensible business decision. An agreement to double tag whatever's around the next corner. Will I still be on the phone when we're septuagenarians, my wrinkled hands typing 'lol, dead' until I'm lol, dead? Forever is ambient. We take each day as it comes.

I know I yarp on about wonderful stuff like the Egyptian Pyramids and the Orient Express and darling you would *love* Cape Town, but ten years into a relationship you don't date in a datey way. There's enough low-key hanging out to fool yourselves you have a spicy life between big holidays. And outside the worldly, well-travelled pomp I'm a surprisingly cheap date. A carbonara literally anywhere is a good time. An obligatory Diet Coke. As a decade-old couple you still do the things that can be termed dates – dinner and a moonie – but you don't stare truly, madly, deeply into each other's eyes for more than a few seconds. You don't flirt outrageously. You don't wonder if you're getting laid. There's a comforting productivity to proceedings, and a commitment to being fed and watered rather than seduced and ravished. You don't really drink too much. You're not coy. And you've developed shorthanded comms. Dot-dot-dashing over dinner.

I've never really been a romantic, so flowers and chocolates have always taken second place to honesty and true security. And I don't mean cash. I mean dependability. That is the good shit. The placebo of romantic offerings always feels a bit naff and insincere. I love a weekend away, I'm very focused on experiences and longevity. We all know a bunch of flowers is dead when it arrives, and I think relationships are for living. I know that weeknight carbonara and a Cairo weekender and a pair of Gucci clogs are not a quiet life by any stretch, but we have a few years before we have kids to resent for keeping us grounded. This is the fallow land before we have toddlers in need of constant wet-wiping. Or tweens with chips on their shoulders. Adolescents with smartphones and free will. Shudder. In the meantime, we're pasta-ing in trainers. These special nights are often the best ones. When we're on vacation we're more like teenagers, there's a sense of occasion, but on a Wednesday in Soho we're feeding ourselves and Ubering home. This is a secure zone where I'm not what I would call my worst self, but there's also zero pressure to be my best self. We're both just ourselves. That's what a decade of dating does.

In the Uber home I check my phone. All our cavities are padded with phone time, like the asbestos insulation in your roof, dormant and toxic and squeezed into the margins of your bloated life. Imagine a film where people actually use their phones like we do in real life, just looking down pretending to listen to each other. Sitting in silence then randomly laughing. Mike Leigh to direct. The thing is, this phone-checking is a dirty habit you keep returning to, not like smoking, because we all agree smoking is bad and even the government is stepping in on that one. A dirty habit more like masturbating to the thumbnails of expensive porn so you don't have to pay for it. It's grim, but you pretend it's fine.

Flesh Tetris

On our first date my husband tricked me. He told me he was Jewish (lie) and he said he'd had a 'back-alley bar mitzvah' (lie) and he then sang the song they had at the bar mitzvah (it was from *The Lion King*, but I didn't twig). I believed him because who would lie about their religion? I was a level of gullible I can only attribute to first-date nerves and the fact that he had (and still has) a Jewish penis. Most of our early dates were at fast-food places masquerading as the new big thing. Remember in 2009 when every new dining experience in London was a sort of chef's frat party, the hosts elevating junk food and trying to out-barbecue each other? In those early days we dated on garage forecourts eating deep-fried soft-shell crab as London's food scene got us to pay £25 for chicken. Looking back, I can't believe it worked – the expensive chicken or the dating of a blatant liar. The thing is, in 2009 you couldn't efficiently Miss Marple who you dated using your phone. You couldn't check up on them by looking at their tagged pictures on Instagram. You couldn't go on your mate's phone and watch their stories. Their locations weren't tagged every other hour. Things were more curated and sporadic, rather than torrential. You had to trust people in the no-man's land between posts. My husband-to-be had about forty profile pictures on Facebook that I carouseled at work trying to figure him out. None of them screamed *Not a Jew*. How was I to know?

After a few dates, we kept bumping into each other while we were out. By accident. It's unfathomable today to imagine bumping into someone randomly on a night out, because we all know where everyone is all the time. Could it be that it was all so simple then, or have apps rewritten every line? Nightlife is drying up. Clubs are closing. Today's app culture makes us indoorsy, like wet play at school when it's pelting outside. We stay inside, sedentary, vying for attention sat on our arses in shoutfits we put together for the camera. You shoot yourself provocatively splayed on the sofa, peacocking from the lounge, rather than the dancefloor. Photograph with no T-shirt on, why you making me wait so long? Like all the exploratory sex of your youth, most things are only kinky the first time, so your pictures get gradually more aggressive, less thinly-veiled, more raunchy. The thirst cut is the deepest, but the illicit thrill fades until you find yourself flinging out nipple pictures like Adderall in expensive colleges, a traffic jam of flesh like tourist gondolas in Venice. Our tolerance for arousal is higher than ever. Expanses of skin have always held allure, so a thirsty Victorian woman could flash a little ankle to get all the boys to the yard. Followed by Britney's midriff. More news flesh than news flash. Paris Hilton heralded the sex-tape era and imagination went out the window. Now we flash our bits digitally in view-once snapshots. Apps have replaced real interaction.

Where dating apps are full of hope, sex apps are full of torsos. Only torsos. The most striking thing on the hook-up platforms is an exacting crop. A chin-to-pudendum sever-ance, a Sahara of hairless flesh like a Google Earth transmis-sion. While in London you're never more than six feet from a rat, online you're never more than six images from a torso, guillotined at the neck like Marie Antoinette if she did a thousand sit-ups a day. We see the valley of a navel and dunes of pecs, but that's about all. No face. No twinkle in the eye. No slight smile on the lips. No tell-tale signs of male pattern balding. Just a torso, *sans* visage. In a reverse of Romeo and Juliet romantically locking eyes through the fishtank, we initially meet via tiles of tanned skin. Star-crossed nipples. Has anyone ever fallen in love with a decap-itated trunk? Our key human identifiers are gone, like a round of applause with no hands. Or sex without using your mouth. These pictures are a constant uninterrupted skidmark of male skin, tessellating together in a flesh Tetris. Torso culture is a continual battery farm of featherless chickens, plucked raw, succulent and perfect.

Ironically, everyone on these apps is asking for face pics, and your reward for initial interaction is a mugshot. But we're set up for disappointment when we venture beyond the perimeter of the armless oblong. When you finally see a full expression, you do the frozen-smile face you always do when you get an off-brand birthday present and have to pretend to love it. Or a novelty present you know is heading straight to landfill. That's a result of the betterment culture where we're submerged, but still searching on a daily basis. Endless scroll suggests endless choice and the idea that something enhanced is round the corner, just out of sight. This guy's face is fine, but I can hold out for hotter. I don't have to settle. The idea of the infinite world beyond our immediate vision keeps us believing there's more for us than what we've already seen. Perseverance will allow us to access and conquer it, like Christopher Columbus.

We can't settle for what's in front of us because we believe something hotter, or at least more optimised is on the periphery. We're convinced we can improve not only the world around us, but our physical and spiritual selves. We can upgrade the people we interact with like clapped-out Nokias. If you were an unpretty gay man in the sixties there was nothing you could do, you were just not a babe. That was your lot. The hot gays patted you on the head and you coupled up with other non-Adonises. Today you don't have to settle, you can just get muscly. The farmable region is from the Adam's apple to just above the pubis. Pump iron and do crunches until the veins in your pecs pop like worms when it's raining. Shoot a well-lit selfie and add your image to the throng of torsos bobbing on the screen like *Titanic* survivors at the end of the film. This is the era of reinvention, of honing and toning, when you can take any part of yourself and enhance it. You don't need a better face for access to a better life, you need the mirage of a great torso to access more lovers. When all discerning features are removed, the belly button is the default window to the soul. This is where the capital of torsos has led us.

Most of the things we love involve some kind of context: someone kissing you on the cheek is nice, but Richard Gere kissing you on the cheek is phenomenal. Mac and cheese is a rainy-day comfort, but Nigella Lawson mac and cheese is a good kind of smack in the face. Although if you want the hot body you're probably avoiding carbs and cheese and you're eating a handful of chicken outside Barry's Bootcamp. I know you're relying on animal protein to build, but you're slowly killing the planet with your carbon footprint. Consider tofu.

Sometimes I'm the Little Mermaid desperate to be part of their world of rigid contoured sixpacks, but sometimes I'm the Jamaican crab Sebastian, satisfied right here on the ocean floor with my belly that's fine when I tense it. I don't want to sound like an over-zealous supply teacher deciding to give an impromptu a lesson on body positivity by asking, 'Would you shave five years off your life for a better body?' I probably would. I'm assuming you're forced give those years up at the end of your life, which is objectively the worst half-decade. You have Alzheimer's and you don't recognise your kids, or prostate cancer but the meds are in Europe and we've left. I'd give up *those* latter-life five years for ergonomic biceps. There will be flying cars but I'll be too old to care, and I'll have had a full life with great thigh cleavage. I'd also give up the five years between right now and having kids, because I suspect it's mainly hospital visits and unviable embryos and soaring heartache and hand-wringing until you're holding a tiny sprog in your placenta-y gloved hands. I'm less keen to lose the first five years of the kid's life, because babies are cute even when they're being sick on you. On the other hand, if we end up adopting we'll get a five-year-old with a name chosen by someone else. Good glutes and a schoolgirl called Janet is a pretty sweet deal, and there's always time to shoehorn a nickname onto her. Click your fingers and you have perfectly toned biceps and a potty-trained pre-teen. Five years in return for instant dilf like a Pot Noodle.

Most apps perpetuate the idea that everyone else is hotter than you. Guys on Instagram come up with most ingenious ways to show off their bodies. You know the accounts: topless guy at the beach, topless guy in the snow, topless guy in a Santa hat, topless guy encouraging you to vote for abortion reform. Flesh is political at a cynically skin-deep level. But meeting these chiselled chaps, like losing your virginity, is always a disappointment. People say celebrities seem shorter in real life, and we're the celebs of our own feeds. Our profiles magnify us, elevating us a few rungs up the ladder, where the air is clearer and our clothes are laundered and we don't snap at our partners when we're stressed. In real life our hair is less full, our teeth less white, our poses less statuesque. We don't have the same cheekbones and we mainly squint because it's the kind of overcast day when you get a headache from squinting. It never drizzles on the feed, the climate is always notable. Feeds are the stage for our life drama. We want the tempest or the Sahara. Unstormy weather doesn't make the cut.

It's impossible to live up to the hype of your digital self and all the noteworthy things you share. You can't be as delectable in the hard light of every day. We all buy into the dream that a pixelated life offers, but it's impossible to keep up with your economical truth. The digital self is a bit like a dick that's always hard – it's great but medically speaking it's a bad thing, a hindrance to normal living, something to trip over while you run normal errands. Nothing is meant to last forever. Eventually it all collapses. We admit defeat to the digital illusion of who we are, and confess our own accuracy like every murderer caught red-handed at the end of every episode of every crime drama ever. All the omissions – the deleted selfies where you have twenty chins, the chronic mood swings, the binge eating, the sitting around all day in sweats when you're not the slightest bit hungover – is who we really are. On a clear day, we can emerge from our cocoon of soft-focus lies, and dispel the beefy mirage of flesh Tetris. We can blinkingly step into the sun, ready to date a fake Jew.

The Fagin of my Friends

Even though I have enough disposable income to buy plates from respectable stores, I'm the Fagin of my friends, smuggling tableware out of restaurants and back to my house. I have cupboards stacked with acceptable plates and casual pasta bowls but I've become addicted to stealing more, a thrill as cheap as red underwear. The rush of adrenalin as the cold porcelain of a Brasserie Lipp dinner plate presses against my skin makes me feel like I've taken ecstasy in the nineties in a rave field in Kent with no tangible plans to get home, just the onward roll of the bassline and bliss. I once left a market diner in east London walking like Terminator 2 because I had six butter knives down my sock. Regardless of the kind of dinner I've had – a quick chopped salad before the theatre, a theatrically-sized pasta at one of those brasseries made predominately of marble, an argumentative main with my husband followed by a passive-aggressive crème brûlée – I steal a plate from the restaurant as a memento, an item to savour the savoury course.

It would surprise you how many places on your person you can secrete a dinner plate when leaving a posh eatery. The front of the trousers is fine if you hunch a bit, or in the rear of your waistband like a porcelain back brace. I once got searched at the gate before a flight and there was an entire KLM breakfast service in my carry-on tote. More than a trinket from the airport lounge, these half-inched plates hold a strange meaning for me. A practical souvenir that instantly upgrades all my snacks because it transports me back to Paris – there's nothing so decadent as cheese and toast off a Chez Janou side plate or M&S ready-soup out of a Colony Grill Room bowl. I tell myself plate-lifting is a victimless crime because restaurants are huge businesses and there are stacks and stacks of back-up plates piled on the stainless steel in the kitchen at the rear. A klutz waiter could smash this very plate next week, I'll say, so I'm actually rescuing it like a Battersea dog.

Plates, for me, are like likes. I don't need the plates. I enjoy them. And I have the same thing with likes on social media. Likes for my wit, mainly, for my personality, which is affirming and makes me feel superior to the torrent of nice outfits and nice faces people say are ruining attention spans and culture and young women's sense of self. It's not that I'm above a selfie. Who among us doesn't know their best angle? But when browsing my selfies of an evening, scrolling back through years of pictures I've taken of myself, existential questions are wont to creep in – *Why am I here? What am I doing with my life? What mark am I leaving on the planet outside of a craterous carbon footprint?* Staring at repeated pictures of the I'm-confused-by-how-handsome-I-am face I do for the camera, I realise the mark I leave doesn't matter as long as the caption on my red-hot selfie has the right alchemy of self-deprecation and wit. Puns make my brags seem humble.

It's all a big distraction, of course. I post the picture as I swipe away news alerts. I post the picture as the country darts down the rabbit warren of Brexit like panicked *Watership Down* bunnies with early-onset myxomatosis. I post the picture as a rich person gets called out for flying in a private jet. And as the Trump administration erases reproductive rights. I post the picture as animals are slaughtered. And children starve. And the Amazon burns. My pores digitally smoothed as Greta Thunberg bobs in the sea waiting for the wind to pick up. Distribution of my own likeness is a distraction from the rolling bad-news cycle. We could save the oceans if we could just stop Instagramming ourselves.

This is an age of unadulterated narcissism; the era of late capitalism is also one of late vanity. Competitive communication around who we are and what we do and how we look clogs all the feeds, our faces reappearing like regurgitated grass in a cow's stomach. A dense custard of selfies and virtuous deeds. Virtuous deeds include caring about the planet and your family and a carbon-neutral job. The most virtuous thing you can do on Instagram is a post damning Instagram for being shallow before you launch into a bit on the climate catastrophe and encourage people to stop eating meat and dairy. I go insane thinking about shopping local. I get the premise: don't buy stuff from far away because of all the air miles and carbon emissions. Sadly, vegetables can't collect points and go on better trips in a better cabin, so the air mileage means nothing. They can't collect Nectar points or Boots points either. Being a vegetable is expensive, with no tax breaks, and I don't believe they're even allowed to peruse Chanel hand cream in the duty-free hall. So, shop local please. My mum lives in this town in West Sussex where they sell *Shop Local* tote bags, which is admirable as the town goes plastic-bag free. But in the same shop they also sell bananas. Bananas are not local produce of West Sussex, because they don't grow well in a climate of torrential drizzle. So not using plastic bags and not eating bananas is virtuous. Be sure to post about it.

Most of us can sniff out disingenuous virtue-signalling like the velociraptors in the kitchen at the end of Jurassic Park. Yet we all want to ascend to a virtuous life, saying things like 'My body is so amazing at getting me from A to B, I don't care what size it is, it's such a magnificent trick of nature and evolution that I'm even here, what's all the fuss about being smaller or taller or less spotty?' Those people are the worst. *We* are the worst. Pretending to casually reflect on our own amazingness. Life is just happening while we saunter along being cool about it all. This is horseshit, Rose, but we want to assimilate.

Every time we achieve, we broadcast. Every stolen plate and uneaten banana. We're all patting ourselves on the back.

Foam-fingering our attributes and drawing attention to everything we do. In return for signalling our own greatness we get liked by our peers, and in an ideal case complete strangers adore us too. We call this fame. The subtext of every post is *Notice me*, and the subtext of every like is *Sure thing*. Likes have a variety of impetuses, but the result is the same: validation. Everyone secretly wants to be liked to a certain degree, even people like me who think they're above such trivialities. And I find myself liking posts and commenting affirmations of positive gibberish on other people's posts as a way to pay it all forward. At some point expecting the positivity to boomerang back. All of us join this precession down the Venetian canal of social media, our smiling carnival masks hiding our true feelings while we tell each other we look great. We catapult likes out across the universe anticipating a return to sender. We give and receive likes in a digital 69. A circle jerk of double taps.

As a true narcissist, when I look at your face in your selfie I think only of my own, and suddenly I can't believe how young I'm not. I didn't realise that in the gulf between being a young person and an old person there's just years of looking tired. Just plain old tired. A reverse Berocca: you on a not very good day. Years of looking not quite your best, like you woke up late and forgot to moisturise, but in reality you slept well and *did* moisturise. I've never been too fussed about looking old. But I thought the journey to elderliness was a quick layover. I wasn't ready for the M25 traffic jam of looking clapped out while you Google subtle surgeries. That was not on my roadmap at all. I thought ageing was as instant as the prosthetics Nicole Kidman wears in *The Hours* or Winona Ryder at the end of *Edward Scissorhands*. I didn't realise ageing was so … gradual. A Chinese water torture of dripping wrinkles. Of course I look smug in my online avatar because it's a Dorian Gray painting of me from a cute angle. It will never change. This might be the only silver lining of online living and spending so much time cultivating a channel. You reap the selfies you sowed when you were younger.

Outside of realising you're ageing, the internet is awash with two types of people: the likeable and the detestable. It's a societal seesaw with no real middle ground. The middle is where people forget your name and your face, sometimes looking right through you like colourless Murano glass. The middle is anonymous, which is only handy if you're a restaurant critic with plates to steal. Pick an end. The likeable are very likeable, they signal virtue well, and if you *can* see the signalling charade it barely fazes you, like body-temperature tea getting spilled in your lap. The likeable are palatable and friendly, and the type of person who'll make trays of personally iced cupcakes for the bake sale. They Instagram those Advent food-bank boxes every day until Christmas, and we all allow it because it's the right thing to do. They have strong and stable bodies, eating food that is both worthy and nourishing. Suckling on organic grapes and gorging on good-quality gouda. They could easily be your friend in the slightly righteous way you can just about stomach. Most people on the BBC are likeable. Think *Blue Peter* or Tess Daly or the head girl from your school (the blonde one). Likeable people thrive off being nice and polite and never swearing or slurring their words or trying to get laid as the sun comes up at 5 a.m. at a stranger's house somewhere in De Beauvoir. They might do drugs, but never in excess. Never calling in sick and watching *This Morning* in a comfy jumper eating Pringles. Never spiky or difficult, the likeable are smooth and accessible, like a good sex toy. They are also a teensy bit grating, but that's just your jealousy talking. Allow niceness. Allow likeability. It's fine. Let it wash over you like lukewarm tea.

As a society we love to keep women on their toes, lest they get too comfy and concentrate on living life rather than projecting a sunny, agreeable and available disposition 24/7. So women are often criticised for not being likeable enough, which basically means unappetising. Imagine not being the kind of woman people want to gobble up. The horror of it. Women are expected to be quietly and delicately palatable, like a Ladurée macaron. Consumable by society at large. Not even sexual, just available. Receptive – no, thankful – to anyone who approaches them. Porous to advances. This whole thing makes me feel stabby. Unless you're a Victorian in a corset and bustle, you know this is an unacceptable double standard. Being likeable is something women contend with, while men just barge forward smashing into everything like a bull in a china shop (which, incidentally, is why restaurants have so many backup plates). Likeability for men can be a weakness, an unnecessary pit stop during the grand prix of ball-breaking and go-getting. Being likeable is sightseeing on the way to the keynote at the conference. Glimpsing the Leaning Tower en route to somewhere more important. Men get to be charming. An otherworldly energy that takes you beyond polite. You can be ever so polite and lack charm. You can be all pleases and thank yous but devoid of genuine charisma. Polite is the earth, charming is the stars.

Likeability and detestability are polar opposites, and hate is a magnetic north. I can tell you the names of two people who hate me and I think of them often, what they're doing and if they're thinking about how much they hate me at the same time I'm thinking of them. I perversely enjoy the feeling of being hated – it's like picking at a scab. My self-esteem is attacked like the engine that birds fly into in *Sully*. Hate doesn't bring self-esteem down, but the pilot feels the turbulence. The people who hate you take all the things you represent and decide they're not for them. They see who you are, they expose it, and they opt out. Their equation of who you are is correct, but they got the answer wrong. A minus, not a plus. The people who hate me could list the reasons why I'm a piece of shit, and I would just nod. They hate me for valid reasons and know my character. They know my truth. That's why it rankles. That's why emotions run so high with exes: because it's not an *idea* of you they negged. It's not some distant projection – they know you well, and they don't want you. You can cushion yourself with the idea that outsiders don't really know you, so they don't matter.

Strangers are much more manageable because they're easier to brush off.

Of course, there's the unlikeable strain of humanity, an Ebola creeping through the veins of the internet. The detestable biker gang, but instead of Harleys they have keyboards. Piers Morgan is Buttons injected with a keg of angry lard, and the insidious jingoist Katie Hopkins from *The Apprentice*. You get a bunch of attention if you're a prick online. Attention for your big mouth and brittle morals and hierarchy of who deserves what. Your indifference to tragedy is notable. You're either trolling celebrities or doing shouty rants about immigration. Loudly bemoaning Meghan Markle's behaviour but never actually mentioning her race. Asking about Hillary's emails or Obama's birth certificate. Calling people in need maggots. Ladling hate over the coals of the sauna of the internet, meaning the temperature rises for everyone and we all get hot and bothered. Our attention-grabbing culture has created a cycle of outrage adjacent to the breaking news. The detestables are massive spoons that stir things up. Nothing is off limits. Paedophiles, terrorists, immigrants. Conflations of all three. The rich, the poor, Parliament, Brussels. Bang bang he shot me down with a savage take on the migrant crisis. We remember the bitter taste of bile, almost savouring it. These people create outrage, and we're outraged by the manic frenzy of their followers. Everyone is at boiling point, or has become completely complacent about it. Our outrage is a tool to monetise our fear.

When I was a plateless teenager I didn't pretend to like people. I was happy to be standoffish. And disagreeable. And a touch contrary. This was before the internet, so the only record of me being so surly is in the memories of my mum's friends. At an age when I was figuring out combat trousers, being too nice to people felt alien to me, like how babies operate. Being disagreeable felt like a form of anarchy against all the polite fakery. Not saying please felt like a micro-rebellion, I guess. I don't know who I thought I was rebelling against. My fair and generous parents, those monsters. My nice teachers who listened to me. Being fake-nice to teachers is social currency at school. I still think of 'head girl' as a slur because it means you succeeded in gaming the asymmetric *like* systems that are played out in schools. Black boys don't often get to be head girl, and this was years out from President Obama, who everybody liked. But politeness and palatability are bigger than the class-room. There are the media-trained butter-wouldn't-melt pop stars. Or the actors doing rehearsed anecdotes. Presenters beaming through hellish broadcasts with those buttery pop stars. Celebrity Robots™ politely bleeping out press releases while everybody says how lovely they are, how humble. You have a very small pool of things you can control and influence as a teenager. The words that come out of your mouth are your only real power after you conquer your bowels as a toddler. Disagreeability is a form of control. Unfortunately, rather than a revolutionary, being contrary only signals you out as a dickhead.

I started smoking when I was thirteen because body autonomy is a form of political protest against an unjust system, and I needed something to occupy my hands between wanks. I wasn't bored or kamikaze or pressured by a gang of non-head girls. I guess I saw people smoking in films, but at that point in the nineties it was *de rigueur* to get enraged over alcopops being marketed to teenagers. The media got its knickers in a twist over Hooch, while the rest of us drank red wine in three-swig passes and took up smoking. Smoking is, and always will be, very, very romantic and dashing, giving the appearance of a *laissez faire* approach to one's own death. People are magnetically drawn to us smokers, because you can smell the mystery just under the carcinogens. We, the puffers, have multi-storey daring, the swaggering buccaneers of the modern age. We're like non-smokers but we don't bother to shower every day and always dodge train fares and play the guitar but not in an achieving-a-grade way, in a cool way. Smokers make better lovers – I guess we have more accuracy, because we want to finish up and have a fag. Smoking is the same as a thigh gap: we all know it's wrong, but still.

For sixteen years I smoked like a chimney and I loved it, but it started to lose its appeal when I was always skint and sick in the winter despite mainlining vitamin-C drinks. Smoking alone on a rainy day walking to university is less gallant than you'd imagine. You're damp and you smell. You feel dumb because any decision you made at thirteen is dumb. It's an age when you have no frame of reference outside of pocket money for chores, but you decide to get addicted to cigarettes.

I talk like I'm still a smoker, but I'm not still smoking. The week before I turned thirty I went to see a hypnotist, who weirdly didn't wear a turban or have lightning bolts coming out of his fingers. He didn't even use a pendulum to put me into a trance, disappointingly. And not even a hint of levitation during the session. He made me stare at my hand forever and then said 'You're under' and fed me loads of mini-mantras about my rampant smoking years, preparing me for my emergence from his hypnotic chrysalis into a nicotine-free adulthood. A butterfly with less yellow teeth. At one point I had to visualise myself as a vulnerable baby in the womb and forcibly shove a cigarette into my own innocent baby-mouth. Despite being a cynic about nearly everything, I'm soft when it comes to learning experiences or actions that might lead to a great anecdote, so I went along with the whole process, metaphorically *foie gras*-ing my foetus self. The most annoying thing is that it actually worked. I left the appointment and dropped my Lucky Strike Blues in a bin and never smoked again.

I quit smoking the same way I gave up being contrary: because neither of those things seemed important when I really stopped to think about them. I guess in my own way I'm en route to being my own brand of head girl, who's likeable and doesn't smoke and reports malicious tweets. I wonder if I'll ever completely grow out of wanting to be liked. Or double-tapping your crap selfie. Or even Faging-ing plates from under the noses of restaurant staff. Although if I did, there'd be nothing to eat off.

What if Jennifer Aniston Isn't Sad?

(And Everything Else that Goes Through my Head in a Yoga Class)

What if Jennifer Aniston isn't sad? She's the poster woman for divorcees and those who don't have kids and has become this reluctant emblem of unmotherhood. We all quietly believe that underneath the sixpack there's suffering, behind the smile there's sorrow, below the calm surface of the Smartwater there are depths of sadness. But what if she loved Brad Pitt and now she's over Brad Pitt? What if she came to terms with the end of the relationship like any normal person and has moved on appropriately, neither too reboundingly soon nor too holding-outily long? What if Jen's had her closure and doesn't want to reopen the wound? What if there never was a wound? What if Brad was the problem? What if Brad's the one who can't let go?

What if every time Paul McCartney sings I wish I'd died with John Lennon so I didn't have to endure solo Paul? What if John was still here and had to deal with internet trolls and the nineties? Would he have gone to Michael Jackson's funeral? Would Yoko have mellowed? What if Diana never got in the car in Paris? Who would she be dating now? Would she have liked *Sex and the City*? Would she have had a Carrie signature necklace but saying 'Diana'? I feel like Diana and Angelina Jolie would've hit it off, clambering over landmines in the Third World in sleeveless linen. Would Diana wear floral Ganni dresses? She'd certainly live somewhere hot and be both noxiously private and somehow still clamouring for attention. Think panic room with a tropical climate and 24/7 butler service. Would she go to the Met Gala every year? Would she have the bulimia under control? Would she be the people's princess or would she be a naff ex-royal like Fergie, all pearls and squandered opportunity? God, the Queen would be livid. I feel like Prince Philip would've 'accidentally' run Diana over by now like Brian Harvey reaching for a baked potato.

What if everyone who responded to your Facebook invite actually comes to the party and all your work colleagues have to mingle with your school friends? What if you have one of those parties that gets out of hand and ends up in the *Daily Mail*? Legendary and massive, the Studio 54 of your little town for one night, but on Monday you have to explain to your boss how the intern came to do heroin in the downstairs loo.

What if by constantly expressing myself on and offline I've lost the most powerful tool known to man: mystery? What if I'm without enigma? People want mystique. Where's my allure if I'm always typing and shouting? I'd love to be thought of as oblique and expensive, but I'm loud and cheap. I'm giving it all away like they tell you not to do in sex education at school. What if I say so much that it's impossible to absorb a single pertinent point? Am I an onslaught of gibberish? What if I'm slowly wearing away my husband with this verbal diarrhoea? The ocean eroding his cliffs. I'm a tit full of milk that has to express whether you want to feed or not.

If God was one of us, would He use apps? Would He order Deliveroo? If He descended from the heavens to earth, would He become an influencer and get us to buy bibles and aesthetically pleasing tunics? Maybe He'd do a podcast sponsored by frankincense. Does he want us all to be carpenters like Jesus? Tune in to find out.

What if everyone had to be gay for a week? Like National Service but bum stuff. You'd get packed off on one of those hideous gay cruises like a war evacuee but the uniform is abs and Speedos. Being straight is fraught with complexities, all toxic masculinity and gendered colours. Women tend to smell like petals, a bath you've put all your smellies into at once. Although it's unlikely, what if I survive the apocalypse, waking up twenty-eight days later, and the only other person left alive is a woman and we have to procreate? Could I do my duty to continue the species without gagging?

What if the worst things are secretly the best? What if Emma is the best Spice Girl? And Theresa May the best prime minister? What if the discontinued Coffee Creams were the best Quality Street? And Hufflepuff the best house?

What if the best things in life aren't free? What if they cost money? And time and energy? What if I book a holiday but don't buy any new clothes for it? What if I look at a Monet without Instagramming it? What if I privatise my life like National Rail? Will it run more efficiently?

What if we're all only pretending it's what's inside that counts? What if spiritual wellness is an illusion peddled by hippy idiots who think trepanning is a legitimate panacea? What if my aggressive spiritual-replenishment regime doesn't work? What if I keep buying crystals but my happiness plateaued ages ago? Will bigger crystals help? What if eating three raw cloves of garlic a day isn't a personality? I once made hummus with so much garlic it got an ASBO. What if you don't mention the other gay men you know within seconds of meeting me? What if I'm something other than my sexuality? What if I'm wrong when I keep saying to my gay mates that they shouldn't use their charm and charisma just to get laid? What if that's why charm and charisma were invented? What if I wasted my most supple years abstaining from casual sex? What if I can't get through the chorus of 'Baby Boy' without remembering that Sean Paul is a homophobic piece of shit? What if I want to navigate my gayness by cherry-picking from all culture, not just the gay bits? I'm over twenty-five, which in gay years is dead. And I've been with my husband ten years, which in gay years is millennia, essentially all the way back to the gays of Ancient Rome in easy-access tunics. I don't want to talk about my dick, but in gay inches it's a leg. Should I just embrace all the gay stuff? What if my dying wish is that I'd joined in and watched *Will and Grace*? What if the clichés in this paragraph are as unsurprising as the moment at a gay party when someone touches your thigh? I call this the dick-twitching hour, when everyone's loins sober up and hedonism gives way to humping.

I like reading, but what if I stop trying to be well-read? I don't think I'll ever be well-read the way Margaret Atwood is well-read. Most people have read *Jane Eyre*. I haven't. I Netflixed *Emma* with Gwyneth Paltrow but I was on my phone the whole time. There's a specialism to being a reader. A football person can explain the offside rule in the same way that a fashion person can explain how something is cut on the bias. A book person can effortlessly retrieve a book moment from memory at a dinner party, sparkling like wine. Can I really write a book while being so blatantly unbookish? Unable to speak from the libraries of my guts. Trying to shoot from the hip of knowledgeable but I've only read *Not Now, Bernard* and *Gone Girl*. What if I can't tell you anything about *Jane Eyre* or Shakespeare?

What if I don't eat all the bread before the starter comes? What if I'm never Russell-Tovey-would-date-me hot? What if I'm never Owen-Jones-would-date-me politically minded? What if I'm never Ben-Whishaw-would-date-me emotionally introverted and artistically extroverted? What if I'm just not one of the biologically elite, and that's OK? Am I swimming upstream against my genes? What if I die from exhaustion?

What if I'm currently living with a rare undiagnosed disease, and eventually I die from it, and I'm the first person to have it so they name it after me? See how my death also became a branding opportunity? When I die from Raven Syndrome, what if no celebrities come to my funeral? What if there's no day of national mourning? What if it doesn't even make the local news? What if my nearest and dearest are secretly relieved they don't have to deal with my shit any more? What if my autopsy report shows semen in my stomach and there's a *Silent Witness*-type investigation until the DNA results come back and it turns out the semen is my own? When I die, please remember that I was trying to be hot. Please commission paintings so flattering people don't quite recognise me, like Elizabeth I. What if in hell you have to eat all the single-use plastic you needlessly used while alive? Or what if there's nothing after we die? I scream, you scream, we all scream for eternity into the void because God is dead. What if my heart doesn't go on?

Notes from the Brink

Regardless of what I'm doing with my day – fretting about macro-nutrition, accidentally offending a good friend, realising I don't have the self-esteem for these trousers – I find myself looking forward. To the evening. To the weekend. To a week's holiday I've whinge-negotiated with my husband. To some distant moment when I'm not working flat out or being a total grump. A North Star of relaxation to sail towards. I crave breaks like pregnant women crave sit-downs and chalk sandwiches. Being on the verge of cracking up is a key signifier of success, and we all seek out remedies that pull us back from the brink of exhaustion. Nowadays I'm a deep-tissue massage with additional cupping away from defecating in the aisle of my local supermarket, but detangling the stress curls of the everyday used to be an easier endeavour. Saturdays were lunch with the girls and a bit of shopping in town. GHD-ing your hair poker-straight as the National Lottery played in the background. The ceremonious donning of your high-street gains and then out into the bitter night, face painted, body waxed, probably drinking a

Hooch. Dance a bit. Do a shot. Kiss someone hotter than your ex. Kebab. Cab. Home.

With mindfulness and gong baths and ayahuasca we're all seeking out a way to switch off, or at least dim, the incandescence of modern living. Anyone with a Muji diffuser can down cashew milk and align their chakras. Devotion to restorative therapies verges on the religious. I don't want to cast myself as the Jesus character, but I'm a true believer in myself. A devout disciple of own abilities, although I would struggle to explain exactly what they are. My CV list on LinkedIn brags, but lacks the nuance of the ongoing romance I've had with myself my entire life. The certainty changed when I left my office job and went freelance. My reasonably cushty role, creating and consulting on short film, pivoted to something where my voice goes straight into your ear rather than scenes in a film on a digital platform or a content strategy. *My brain in a business* became *My voice in your ear*. There's no more hiding in teamwork. My vision isn't being translated through a director's lens, or a social team's unanimous edits. It's just me and you, with no condom of protection between us. You're currently barebacking my voice, so thank you. Intimacy is terrifying and exposing and I'll take any suggestions on how to receive mild criticism without spiralling into self-abusive thought patterns and binge drinking. With immediate delivery come inevitable waves of doubt.

What if I'm not a snack, but the whole damn meal, and everyone gets indigestion? What if I'm not a slice of cake as a treat, but a three-tiered wedding cake with double layers of icing and over-sweetened pouring cream? What if I'm too sickly? What if I like meeting new people purely because everyone I've known a long time quietly thinks I'm annoying? What if none of my friends proper like me either? What if they talk about me behind my back, discussing the myriad issues of their gobby friend? What if friendship is more of a historic rivalry, a bit like a cousin you can't shake? What if every WhatsApp group is a false security blanket that makes you think you're supported by your friends, but you never have to see them to put it to the test? The phantom thread only suggests proximity and never really delivers? What if everybody's typing … but nobody's listening?

Putting myself front and centre of my career is hideous and rewarding in equal measure, and the interrogation I once had for an incoming story has become introspective. Sifting through the flour of my own thoughts and trying to bake bread people actually want to eat. I've been screaming at the top of my lungs since I was born, so the surveillance is arduous. My brain chatter is a bit like every scented candle in Liberty's burning simultaneously, as molten wax tsunamis and a cloying smoky residue forms on the ceiling.

I'm evangelical about what I do and the stories I tell, whether they're mine or Beyoncé's or Hamlet's, or the genuine desire to communicate that my cat is special. Culture is a bloody abattoir and I'm a butcher, which might sound aggressive for a wannabe pescatarian, but a butcher has confidence. You can't shank a shank without confidence.

You can't gut a pig or filet-o-fish. You need a certain bravery to get into the guts of a thing. Confidence is insulation that gets you from cradle to grave without falling into the side ditch of self-loathing. The stoic belief that my perspective is worth hearing. I have to get bloodied up to the elbows and trust that something digestible will be served before the meat turns rancid. It's the same as amateur night on New Year's Eve but I'm prepared. I have party feet in my shoes and I had a glass of milk with my dinner.

Being a disciple of yourself is like any religion really: there's no science or proof to back up the blind faith. There are a few clues you're doing amazing sweetie, but nothing definitive. You just disproportionately believe in *you*, and in something bigger than what you can feasibly achieve, repeatedly punching above your weight. In laboratory conditions the measurements don't tally because the total is greater than the sum of all the parts. There's no physicist from a movie, nodding his or her head conclusively in a white lab coat in front of a blackboard scribbled with unintelligible equations. You just trust, in the same way we all believe water's good for us or that there's something after we die. You can't shrug off life's free radicals and swerve the potholes if you don't believe. You have to drink the Kool-Aid of your own life. You have to completely commit to whatever it is you do. To see the nooks and crannies of it and never scoff. Outsiders scoff. There are no half-measures. No half-careers. You have to believe in what you do with cult-like evangelicalism. Cynicism will stop you in your tracks. Cynicism is the enemy. Does this all sound a bit Scientology? Doubt is a suppressive thought that hinders your success. Perhaps my next career move is becoming a cult leader. I've always fancied myself as a messiah. I'm partial to mint green, so the disciple robes would be iconic – think Pete Postlethwaite as Friar Lawrence with a dash more hair and quite a large sunhat. Obligatory Birkenstocks. I haven't really thought beyond the outfits, but I could read some Philip K. Dick and get the ball rolling on a credible manifesto.

The worst thing about a real career is that you have to hang out with people you don't like. A makeshift family where everyone's sucking up to the boss. A commune with a monetary objective. Irritating people at the next desk with smelly lunches. Let's call them colleagues. If you want a moment's peace you have to get on with them. A sunny disposition isn't a construct, exactly, but being nice to people all the time is unrealistic. Other people can be abrasive, despite their commitment to healing crystals and foldaway commuter bikes. To survive the peopleness of people you develop a persona, which is a layer of artifice that keeps work interactions jovial and shields the real you. A persona is protective bubble wrap, a soft commodity. Something malleable for sale rather than carved out of rock. I have completely failed to master the persona trick. I can't conceal my vulnerability like my eyebags. I know what you're think-ing – boo hoo, poor guy, being his authentic self all the time and people respond so well to it – but my God, my life would be a lot easier if I had a persona. If I could separate out the strands like curds and whey. Drop the act on the tube home without the macro-aggression of my colleagues and partymates weighing on me. I'd never sit bolt upright in the middle of the night remembering minor criticisms. It's annoying that my interior world is a constant Crayola, manically scribbling on top of itself as the paper gets darker. It's a beehive of chaotic mass activity that somehow produces honey. I'm the queen bee, the worker, the hive, the honey itself – all of it at the same time. A persona is an exoskeleton that safeguards the existential disarray, but when I'm with other people I know they can see my innards. We all wear masks, metaphorically speaking, but imagine taking off the mask. Something to slip off as you come home like your shoes at your friend's parents' house. Imagine if all this interior and exterior stuff – my relationships with people, my compulsion to express, the scattergun thinking, the need to create – was a cloak that got hung up at night. I'd be able to put down *Raven Smith*, or lock him in the guest bedroom. A timeout for his brain to pace the floor at 1,000 miles an hour thinking of in-jokes for the coastal elite and personal anecdotes that resonate.

A sabbatical from the self would be agreeable. A vacation. Two weeks maybe, or even just a long weekend. Some light relief from the insistent turning of the cogs and analysis of what I like or don't like or want to critique impartially. Time off from waking up and doing voicenotes in my deep, deep morning voice that sounds like I'm trying to be straight at school. I keep listening back to them and wondering if I can do voicework in that tiny morning timeframe before my vocal cords normalise and I sound like myself again. My usual talking voice is as high as a soprano at the opera. As irritating as birdcalls in the morning. It's the froth on a cappuccino. I'm not sure if I like it.

I dream of enjoying culture without the need to examine it, falling into the water of an evening at the opera and letting myself sink without trying to determine the direction of the current and the ease of the swim at a storytelling level. I imagine experiencing something for the experience of it, and the opportunity to like it, rather than to form a comment to express like breastmilk. The foot a little off the gas. Please understand, this isn't strictly arrogance talking: 'Poor me, it's so hard being engaged.' But there's a desire to switch off, to retreat to a cupboard and slump like a puppet or decommissioned robot.

My God complex and my impostor syndrome are forever battling it out like ITV *Gladiators* on Saturday nights. Self-belief and uncertainty smashing into each other like the skin-on-skin conflict in a bareknuckle fight. Climb up a ladder and slip down a snake, because you've earned both. A competition old as time itself, like rock-paper-scissors where each opposition has equal clout. The God in me believes I can achieve anything I want. The impostor knows it's a façade. The impostor knows I'm tricking myself. The two of them function like tectonic plates with friction. You know when you go to a party and someone who hates you is there, and you're basically performing happiness and life-and-soulness for their benefit while also pretending you haven't seen them? I have that, but with myself. The God complex circling the room in a cloud of indelible charisma pretending he can't see the impostor nursing a martini glass of sourness in the corner. We all need a level of denial to survive, to create, to put a part of ourselves on paper and show it to someone else. I want to be brutal with my own sense of Raven Smithness, to look at my traits unflinchingly and grapple with them. I also want to ostrich. I want to bury my head deep into the sand and drown out the noise.

If you have a *Titanic* personality – shiny exteriors and bravado – you're always heading for an iceberg. I scan the horizon waiting for the lurch as the hull collapses. It's not arrogance to see how I can fill a room with myself like a gas everyone inhales. But I have a duty to monitor the Ravenmonoxide, lest the gas turn toxic and we all get poisoned. I remember going to a new friend's party at primary school and her mum saying she regretted hiring a professional entertainer on account of how I was standing in the middle of the room and performing for the whole group like a very well-trained dolphin. Except there was no training. Constantly making it about yourself means you're never quite enjoying anyone else. My New Year's resolution is always to turn it down a notch, but here we are.

I'm a siege of personality, a hostage of myself with Stockholm syndrome. The love–hate relationship always errs on the side of love. I'm the showrunner of my own

Truman Show. The genie and the bottle, trying to rub myself the right way and grant wishes that fulfil my sense of self. You need a little magic to get you through and I'm complicit in my own coercion. Realists are the most depressed for this exact reason. It's hard to like yourself when you're being brutally honest. It hard to like anything really. You have to say you have a *Titanic* personality and let that float out across the sea. Fuck the icebergs. Life is a confidence trick, literally tricking yourself into confidence and pretending you have enough lifeboats.

If you embrace yourself, your too-muchness and your other foibles, people think you're an arrogant prick. If I say I'm great I can hear your back going up. There's a shyness, or maybe a decorum, in British culture about saying 'I've worked hard and I own the work and I'm proud'. Cut to me in short shorts in Covent Garden: I worked on my thighs and now I love my thighs and here are my thighs. The British have to pretend our achievements just happened while we were taking high tea between foxhunts. P.S. Being chill about hunting is the most British-upper-class thing ever, and I suspect they'd cull common people too, given half the chance. Everyone is waiting for external validation, on and offline. Waiting for more likes. Waiting for Trinny and Susannah to say 'Nice tits.' Anyway, if you've worked on your legs, show off your legs. Embrace the persona of the short-skirted. Fill every room with your benign oxide like an AirWick plug-in that soothes rather than suffocates.

If, like me, your personality has stopped snuffing out the people next to you like a *Midsummer Murder*, take it out for a spin. Take it to the bar. Take it out for cocktails. Own your personality. Like the speaker I bought with Amazon gift cards in the January sales, your personality has huge value but didn't cost you that much. Acknowledge your faults (yawn) and then act like those nutty women in magazines who marry themselves. Start from the bottom: exfoliate, moisturise, masturbate. Take yourself on a date (this can just be to your kitchen). Chat yourself up. Laugh at your own jokes. It's very Oprah to assail your own personal pedestal without the safety rope of self-deprecation.

I don't want to sound too self-helpy, but if you actually like yourself and register your faults, the dread of being found out as an impostor lessens. You're less forever-anxious about saying the wrong thing. You can still be a god, but a human one that has normal experiences and interactions with other people. Wait, that's Jesus. OK, after you date yourself be like Jesus. There's a cure for leprosy now, but every house party needs water turned to wine. A God complex needs a dash of bitters. So Jesus yourself and leave an unapologetic mark on this sodding planet. Jesus was inclusive. I know he got angry about the Del Boys trading in the temple, but he once fed 5,000 people at one sitting. For me, I know I can raise the temperature of a room, rather than just burning as bright as I can on the spot like a Catherine wheel while everyone stands back at a safe distance. Caring for other people means monitoring your output, not lessening it, and channelling that energy into an atmosphere.

Doubt always creeps back in. *What if the way I act at parties is actually a flamethrower that singes the eyebrows of everyone I come into contact with? What if I never notice? What if I have the hardy courage of the Lion in* The Wizard of Oz *so I'm able to smash through any shindig with pizzazz, but I'm brainless like the Scarecrow? Like, properly emotionally dumb? What if I've read the room completely wrong? I'm stripping at the kids' party. I'm tap dancing at the wake. And I'm too loud and brash to realise I'm acting like a prick. If all the pictures from the night look cute, will I just carry on? How do I stop if I want to stop? Do I want to stop?* When these thoughts reach full capacity it's time for that sabbatical. Like all relationships, the one with the self mellows. Dramatic dating gives way to quieter leisures, the goal being mental stealth.

In the meantime I've stopped punishing myself for being fun, and stopped my pursuit of fun being something that punishes other people. The realisation came as a relief, to be honest, like making peace with a sworn enemy before you die. The enemy wasn't an enemy after all. It wasn't an issue to tackle. Not something to fix, but something to own. Something to accept. My yoga teacher once said, and I found it to be true, that a rising tide lifts all boats. I want everyone in the flotilla. Nobody gets drowned out.

Will I Be a Good Dad?

My life is an unpaid internship. A tessellation of thankless home-tasks that stack up like honeycomb. I don't get paid for Ocado-ing or sweeping, or maintaining a cross-house light system using only eBay-sourced Bauhaus lamps. Compulsively monitoring the sell-by dates in the fridge to avoid food poisoning falls outside my day rate, and I de-weed the front garden for free. I appear to have married a chap oblivious to clutter, a serial untidier, an international man of mess-tery. There's something silently infuriating about having to redo everything I've already done. A Groundhog Day of domesticity. Plugging my phone back in. Putting my washing back in the washing machine. Amending the avalanche of dry pellets that overfeed the cat. Shoving the Fairy liquid towards the sink. Seeing my phone unplugged again. Returning the eggs to the carefully chosen piece of marble where we agreed to keep the eggs. Returning his shoes to the place we agreed to keep his shoes. Plugging my phone back in, so help me God.

Somehow my husband's stuff settles on every surface, like truffle shavings in a posh restaurant. We've assigned a husband cupboard for his life sundries, but it's full and if you open the door the kitchen is flooded with a cascade of unrecycled A4 paper and his autonomous purchases that I've deemed too unaesthetic for public display. There's a dining chair that slowly submerges under his autobiographies of successful capitalists which I regularly syphon off into the life-sundries cupboard. And don't get me started on the puddle of near-identical grey trainers that creep out across the bedroom floor like large woodlice devouring floor space. It kills me to come home to him sitting at the kitchen table with the big light on, rather than the aforementioned Bauhaus lamps.

My husband has other skills outside of the mundane labours of modern life. He's more of an I-completely-sorted-out-the-mortgage-negotiations-darling-and-of-course-I-noticed-your-new-haircut-I-was-just-about-to-say kinda guy. This is an invaluable marriage-enhancing skill, but I can't shake-and-vac away my resentment every time I have to plug my fucking phone back in. Like Thatcher-time miners I go on strike to try to force my husband to pitch in, but he honestly does not see the odd jobs. He's blindfolded to them, like sexy pirate cosplay with two eyepatches, but it's not sexy. He can't see my placard scrawled on the back of a John Lewis box. *Never knowingly under-protested.* When you're on strike you waltz round the house pretending you can't smell the bin or see the recycling spilling over and that the weeds in the front garden are a bohemian feature.

I know my striking is a retaliation to a workload I imposed on myself. We've started the process of having kids, and I can't shake the feeling that striking with a toddler is a bad idea, that opting out of the demands of an infant has results like malnutrition or those bowed legs you get from rickets. I think of scurvy as a swashbucklingly romantic disease, the consequence of an adventurous life on the open seas where you can't stop for vegetables on account of the mass skulduggery. But imposing scurvy on a child seems intense and irreversible, like poking an ex on Facebook, or drilling a hole in an antique. Me and my tornado-of-mess husband curling out kids has a sense of adventure, until I stop to really think about their impact on our lives.

As someone who stopped eating poached eggs because I didn't have the patience for the controlling of the temperature of the water, or the swirling whirlpool thing, or the attention to timing and blotting, I worry about becoming a father. Parenthood, I've heard, needs bottomless patience, which is difficult to balance with my ingrained sense of efficiency and productivity. My slightly piratey high-seas 'If you're not moving forward, where are you going?' mantra doesn't translate to a baby who can't walk yet and keeps shitting itself. It's tricky to look a baby in the eye while saying, 'If it takes less than two minutes, do it now.' Email rationales don't work on newborns.

I've always leaned towards immediacy as a personality trait, and thought all the other frayed parts of my ego would cauterise once I had a kid. In the delivery room all my stroppiness would transfer into the placenta before we sold it off to Harrods women in pill form, and all the unnecessary grumpiness would steep into the birthing pool, to disappear when we pulled out the plug. Our act of childbirth would signify my own rebirth, emotionally scrubbed up like a new penny. I would leave the Lindo Wing (yes, the Lindo Wing) with my child burritoed in my arms and a mood-swingless personality, with bucketfuls of stamina for the challenges ahead. My usual air of chronic dissatisfaction and insoluble irritation, coupled with a constant fear of debt, didn't scream procreate, but look closely and you can see the steely determination of my new, more balanced life.

And I read that kids are like sponges, soaking up your mood like a French baguette on carbonara dregs. Your issues stain them like an orange bolognaise tidemark on Tupperware. Is chronic dissatisfaction the bad kind of infectious? Or is it quite fortifying for modern life? Is the human condition, on the whole, a touch disappointing? Isn't it better to know that before you turn three? Why wait for adolescence for your dreams to come crashing down? A few years ago my husband said, 'A kid won't make you more patient and less selfish' (ouch), and that's something I've been working on ever since. Patience is more than a virtue. Waiting for things without becoming a tight ball of knotted frustration is the new goal. How long can you queue at the self-service checkout before glancing at your watch and calculating how many days you realistically have before your death? Time is a factor. I feel like I'm running out of it, in a way my parents don't, though they're statistically closer to death. This fear of not moving and not building all the time is the product of our optimised, efficient era. Patience is the final frontier of our see-now-buy-now quagmire.

We all want convenience. My hobby is deleting and re-installing the apps I've decided take up too much of my time and deter me from the righteous path of fatherhood. There's no greater power than the power of goodbye, waving off the time-wasting applications like a tray of champagne flutes at a wedding reception, which I'll also be doing because I'm the one dropping the babysitter home after the event. I want to eat well so Deliveroo is banished. The hours between meals pass pleasantly, but then I get hungry and my organic, probiotic aspirations waver. The chickpeas need a ninety-minute boil *after* you soak them all night. The celeriac needs an hour in the oven. The baby has finally cried itself to sleep. And in two taps the app is back, fleetingly useful again. The kilojoules I've burned deleting and re-downloading Deliveroo could power the Blackpool illuminations. That's an exaggeration, but they could power at least a couple of dozen baby monitors. It's funny how I can identify the things in my life that are wasting my time and distracting me from the bigger picture: my real, focus-and-it-can-happen goals. My children will need to be fucking savage to steer my attention away from my apps. The lengths they'll need to go to to surpass Instagram in my esteem. Homeware percussion is an unwelcome intrusion, but their attention-grabbing strategies will become more extreme. Casual racism. Voting Tory. The little Katie Hopkinses of our home.

The convenience and accessibility afforded to us by apps have made us complacent and removed from the real-life processes that keep us in leather shoes and woolly jumpers and cute little babygrows. With apps we no longer have to do anything. Ever. Apps for when you're hungry. Apps for when you're heathy. Apps for when you're lonely. Apps for when you're horny. Apps for when you want to watch people you hardly know renovate their houses. Apps for when you've spent too much time on your phone. I've never looked at any parenting apps, but I assume they're either annoyingly righteous or savagely slummy. Where's the app for normal people with offspring? Where's the app for surrogacy couples with no patience? Patience is a key skill when you start surrogacy, because women who want to devote up to eighteen months of their time and their body to you are nothing like buses. Hardly any ever come along.

Most people want to be great parents, which is cute but on the whole impossible. Trying to be an inspiring person is futile. Generally speaking, you have to be your best self and let other people take from that what they choose. It's impolite to force inspiration on someone, in the same way it's frowned upon to trick a vegan into eating chicken stock. Good parenting is a mirage, like chicken fillets in a bra.

For many, the pressure to be an excellent parent is greater than the pressure to keep their small people fed and watered, which is all they really need. Thank god I won't have to take a stance on breastfeeding. I love coming at parenthood from a place of complete theory, like my conceptually heroic actions when aliens finally attack. The problem with theories is that they're pure fantasy and tend to disappoint, like losing your virginity. I want to be the parent who has everything slowly baking in a clay pot while my husband does scrambled eggs in the microwave. I'm not down with microwaves. I want Nigel Slater eggs – silky, buttery, adjective-laden ova muddled over a naked flame in a country-style kitchen in central London while Radio 4 plays. And Mrs Dalloway flowers. And underfloor heating. Trying to raise offspring in a house without underfloor heating is a form of child abuse.

Home grown plant-based eating is an inconvenient chore, like smiling at your neighbours. Despite the waffle iron I've used no more than three times, I'm still sure I could keep a few chickens in the garden and gather their eggs for breakfast. But what if I want a kiwi? What if a kiwi is the only thing that will get me and my arsehole kids through this miserable Wednesday? Am I going to do a man from Del Monte and pop my linen suit on and go to a hot country where the kiwis are being harvested this week and pick one off the branch and bite into its green flesh as its warm juices run down my chin? No, I'm going to go to Sainsbury's because I don't fuck around. The cornerstones of my personality are a certain sturdiness and some frivolity. That, I hope, is what little people need, rather than some annoying twat who's 'always here to listen when you need it, champ'. Of course I'll always be there to listen, but listening is boring by default. One of the most exciting things about creating new life is knowing you'll be there the first time they eat a McDonald's fry. A human milestone akin to no other. Knowing my luck, I'll probably have vegetarian kids who eventually grow their own sustainable weed in their bedrooms rather than importing coke.

I secretly don't give a fuck about being a bad parent. It's difficult to say that to the very sweet people at the surrogacy agency, because the whole process is like a first date where you pretend your best self is your only self and you don't enjoy the smell of your own farts. I'm not bothered about saying the exact right thing in real life, but at the surrogacy meetings I always want to sound like the kind of cool operator who isn't fazed by the constant assault of modern life. Who isn't on the verge of tears whenever he goes on the tube. Whose favourite recreation isn't watching compilations of people falling over on YouTube. Who definitely doesn't go on strike over housework. I'm ever so slightly paranoid that the expectant mother – the benevolent she-figure who'll incubate our offspring for nine months like a large jar of burping kombucha – will read this book during her pregnancy and do a U-turn on giving us our kid, which in Britain is *completely legal* because the law is fucked. There are more comprehensive books on that subject. Our criteria for her are very lax. As in 'Please don't do hard drugs during the actual pregnancy.' I don't care if she eats sushi or doesn't do Kegels. Be great if she moisturises, but that's more for her.

So kids are coming. Somehow. And we'll have to adapt. I've built a myth around myself that I'm a fast learner, a quick study. I take to things easily because I'm smart and adaptable. Kids are going to extinguish these delusional flames of self-understanding with upchucked milk. How does one adapt to a thousand soiled nappies? I like the implicit idea that my DNA and evolution have prepared me for any significant life processes, but God forbid you catch me in the middle of something I find hard. I'm a nightmare. I'm not a Stepford Wife, exactly (I don't have the fastidious grooming regime), but I'm nailing not completely falling apart at the seams. And despite my feminist principles I secretly hope someone out there refers to me as a trophy husband, based exclusively on my Instagram feed and dress sense. A kid would unravel this trophy image, stealing my precious sleep and exposing the public-facing hallucination of my doing-OK life.

When it gets to talking age the potential for crippling embarrassment magnifies. My husband and I conspire to keep the secrets of our worst selves, but our kid will fuck that up. Kids perform a ventriloquism of your home life. 'My daddies eat biscuits in bed. My daddies don't have indoor voices. My daddy smacked me and my other daddy paid me 50p not to tell you.' I'm excited for little junior to leach away the foundations of my identity, and for me to transition from fun person to parent.

At least with kids I'll have something to chart the passing of time that isn't my Twitter feed or my crows' feet or the unread paperbacks on the dining-room chair. Speaking of paperbacks, kids have godawful taste, all pink plastic and noise. Unsustainable Action Men, bimbo Barbies, tiny but noisy drumkits. Kids aren't very Vitsoe. Kids aren't very Eames. Kids are kind of lowbrow in their tastes. Can I take years of bland food and *Peppa Pig* and wipe-down surfaces? I love a tiny chair, but only on a cute aesthetic level. I don't want my whole world reduced to knee height. The tiny shoes are a big draw. I've always hated having big feet, and kids have default tiny feet and legumes for toes. This is a good thing. Anybody who works with me on a clothing level knows I won't stand for bad-quality outfits, so bankruptcy via teensy cardigans is on the cards.

How many kids to have is a conundrum because of depleting planetary resources and floor space in my actual house. I'd like four, like the *Charlie and the Chocolate Factory* grandparents, so they can tag team my end of life care and I'll always have someone well-rested to entertain me on my deathbed. Like poppers in the pub, brothers and sisters spice things up. When I was growing up a travel Yahtzee and a pirate copy of *The Lion King* were my only siblings. I once won a competition to draw your best friend with a drawing of my teddy bear, which has nothing to do with being an only child, but there you go. Before you reach for the violin,

I'm not complaining. The best thing about being an only child is that you're always the favourite and you never have to compete. You never get dethroned by a screaming little brother or sister, or have them outshine you by doing better at their GCSEs years after you sat yours. There's no real compromise. As a little boy I always got the top bunk. Little has changed.

To an outsider, large families seem incredibly hectic – all middle children and fractured attention and character traits assigned not long after birth. If, for example, you mention in passing that you like cats then you are the cat kid and your whole existence is defined by cat paraphernalia. Cat cakes and cat cards and cat wallpaper and cat clothing. Parents always have a favourite child, much to the dismay of the secondary and tertiary siblings. It's one of those things people hate to admit lest their kids get complexes and hack the inheritance pot, blowing the whole thing on black in Las Vegas. Unfavourite siblings plot to overthrow the sitting prince or princess using passive-aggressive social techniques, much like an office. The hierarchy of birth is a lottery, but if you're not the youngest or eldest you're irrelevant until you do something attention-grabbing, like arson or admitting you don't like cats that much. The siblinged also develop a kind of anxiety about being alone, which I bypassed. Solitude is a comfort for me. Being on my own makes me feel like a Brontë sister, for some reason. Going on long walks and thinking deep thoughts unencumbered by the whims of a big sister with a big mouth. I wonder if I can instil solitude in my own kid by leaving the cot un-attended for a few days? Or just hiding upstairs in the attic when they get back from school? Or going on a month-long cruise and leaving them forty tins and a tin opener?

I want to be committed to my children's education and also quite sexy, like Michelle Pfeiffer in *Dangerous Minds*. I want to impart great pearls of wit and wisdom and life skills that actually matter (whilst maintaining my great hair). Despite a summer learning to be gay in the bushes on Brighton seafront, I've never been particularly good with my hands. I can't draw and I can't paint. I can't play the piano. I've never been able to get my compulsive need for control to translate to my fingers. I can button up a shirt, because I'm not a complete troglodyte. I can rewire a plug and I clawed through AS-Level art with abstract scribbling. I could paint a house if I wanted. Broad strokes never trou-ble me, but the edges are smudgy. A writer, not a speller. A shape-thrower, not a dancer. A loud but tuneless singer. Kids need only some of these skills, if skills is what we call them. I'm a Venn diagram where the expressive circle and the motor-function circle never quite intersect. My hands work just fine, but I can't create a picture of something that you would want to look at. So painters and painting have always enthralled me. Fingers that look more or less like mine, but that can create sublime likenesses or expression of a scene. Hands that reflect the subject with signature flair. Everybody wants to fuck a painter. Painters are the hottest people on the planet. The considered interpretation of the world around them, the grubby hands and forearms, the bouts of creativity with pincer focus. Fuck him more than once and you can call yourself the muse to a creator, the only respite from his insatiable creativity, pressed up against an easel, the smell of white spirit cocooning you from the artless outside world. The boozy whispers of Francis Bacon, the romantically distant (and syphilitic) van Gogh, Vermeer piercing your ear for a pearl earring.

I have a list of baby names ready to go, some of which I've kept secret from my husband so I can 'pretend' to think of them at the birth and he doesn't have time to formulate a proper counter-argument. Naming your children is its own minefield, like the one Diana paraded through in a splashguard. Royals are usually terrible with names. 'Archie' sounds like an American trying to sound quintessentially English, doesn't it? The wrong name can scar a child for life. Too sensible and it's boring. Too artsy-fartsy and they're a laughing stock. Too biblical and there's a plague. Though people tend to grow into big or weird names. Some of us are blessed with names that are all party at the front (Raven) and business at the back (Smith). Perhaps that's a tradition I need to continue. Your pets are great practice for baby names. My cat is called Hastings, because I've had a thing for British places as first names ever since I met a cat called Ipswich as a kid. Also, Hastings is Hercule Poirot's companion which is achingly literary and thoroughly on brand. I want a second cat and I want to call it Dorsia. Evidence suggests that my current cat is besotted with me, but I think his adoration should be put to the test ahead of any children entering the homestead. A second feline presence would mix things up. Since I went freelance and pescatarian I'm home all the time and I smell of fish so I'm human catnip and Hastings takes me for granted. Perhaps I should go on strike. That seems the only suitable course of action before I become a parent and have to finally grow up. Before nappies and the slow erosion of the self. Between surrogacy appointments, I'd enjoy watching the cats battle it out for my affection while I pretend I can't smell the bin.

Aperitivo

And now the final frame. Blockbuster films like to end with the battle-wounded protagonist looking out across a scene – the embers of a flattened cityscape, a suspiciously calm sea – reflecting on the way he's irrevocably changed and grown before the screen fades to black. Bond gets the girl. Poirot fingers the murderer. I, on the other hand, find myself isolated in provincial France during a heatwave, mainlining baguette, my tracksuit bottoms translucent in the seat from living in this chair. As I swallow another cornichon, I'm desperate to do three things. The first is to go home, back to my cat and my husband and the fridge. Secondly I'd like to go out to lunch with my mates somewhere where the food isn't even slightly Gallic. Somewhere with a menu of Union Jack meats and nothing sautéed. Thirdly I'd like overpriced cocktails in a place that has a dress code pretentious enough to roll the eyes. Think Ascot ladies day without the fisticuffs. All three desires are trivial pursuits – hugely meaningful to me but not super significant in the greater scheme of things. Frivolous the second you get a news alert.

A husband is a like a vacation: something you don't make enough space for until suddenly it's the most urgent, overdue thing on the planet. Sometimes you want to get your head down on a project, to lose yourself in the work. But marriage forever hums in the background like aircon, invisibly keeping the atmosphere regulated. And like aircon, you often don't notice marriage until it needs a tinker. I'm thrilled to be heading home, to a Saturday morning with nowhere to go, but more importantly, nothing to write. I might make the cake I got from *The Guardian*, or Ottolenghi's coronation cauliflower. We might illegally stream a film because we can't be arsed to get dressed. Talk will turn, as it often does, to excessive fretting about what we're going to do when the cat dies and whether or not he's had a good life. To that end, I'm still not sure if my cat likes me for me, or if my physical and emotional warmth are interchangeable with those of any other human. Am I just a hot water bottle with a soothing voice? The cat once moved in with my parents and within a week had seduced them into thinking they were special too. No mean feat.

I've missed my friends, though we don't hang out like we used to in our 20s. There's limited mooching. We used to group-watch TV drinking beer, but now things are more event-y. Ballet and a Byron, and the collective Uber affluence that means no night bus. We used to whinge about our flatmates and now we share renovation advice. We spent a lot of time watching TV and making witty asides like twitter in the flesh. We once spent an entire night group-schmoosing an exercise ball. An extrovert Olympics but none of us had work the next day. Nearly every friendship group is a plait of conjoined neuroses and a history of shared achievements and failures. A reciprocal relationship of vulnerability and nurturing with deep pockets of binge-drinking. Most of your mates are dickheads, and I hate to break it to you but so are you. Good friends accept your particular brand of dickhead and aren't waiting for you to change like the hero in the movie. Friendships are just dickhead acceptance with different lengths of backstory.

Good dinners let you binge-eat classic snacks on nicely designed plates and drink sparkling water and lose yourself in conversation before saying yes to pudding. You leave with your palette cleansed, your bouche amused. Before dinner, the sweet-and-sour of the right cocktail is simply a kiss on the mouth, with the promise of all that follows. The tart cameo of an *aperitivo* is a line break in your day, a transition, getting you whet for the night ahead. Instagram delivered me an acquaintance on the Orient Express and I can't shake the thought that with a gimlet and the right shoes I'll be feeling less dog-eared in no time. I'm ready to turn the page on this *aperitivo* chapter, to break the shackles of croissants and go out into the world with some real trousers and shoes that pinch. The donning of discomfort hints at upright proceed-ings. It's impossible to be sedentary when you're buttoned up.

All that throwaway stuff – the beach reads and HIIT workouts and cashew milk and shots of apple-cider vinegar and recycling and sneaky episodes of *EastEnders* – is where the living is done. Birthdays and weddings and funerals matter, of course they matter, but the tracksuit bottoms, and the binge-drinking, and the hidden trans fat is the glue that holds us all together, that's our collective humanity. The commonalities that don't appear to be particularly special keep us connected like limpets on a rock. The tide goes out and our rock pools are separated, but full of the same water.

What have I learned writing this book? I can't allocate the experience as good or bad yet. It just *was*. The cleverer I tried to sound, the dumber I felt. The only time it's cool to sound like a precocious head girl in when you're the precocious head girl. It's harder to make a clear point when you're tripping over enormously extraneous adjectives. Over-chewed paragraphs are flavourless gum. I want the book to be as easily penetrable as a fresher at freshers' week, which is as much a note for my editor as myself. Like most of us, all I know for sure is that I'm tired. Like straight after you workout and you're waiting for your heartrate to stabilise and the endorphins to kick in. I feel like a balloon with the helium sucked out. An empty scrotum of rubber. Or maybe a deflated guest mattress that's more easily refilled. Wait, maybe I'm a KeepCup and I just need a black coffee. That's not very cool, but it's accurate.

If anything, I have to atone for the fact that in real life I'm significantly grumpier than this book suggests. I'm less consistent in the flesh, so this book is me on a good day, before I inevitably shut down because I'm bored or hungry or remember life is finite. It's hard to stay chipper when you realise everything is trivial and you lack any real control over the big stuff. And the chaos has a nasty habit of exploding back into view, pressing at my temples like a sudden sharp migraine. But that's not to say I don't enjoy it. Our attempts to manage our mortality are evident everywhere – fashion, politics, Instagram filters with perfect cheekbones. These are our distractions from death, the smoke and mirrors that stave off our fear of that abyss on the other side of being alive. It's all just a big cope. Instead of running through the streets tearing out clumps of hair and bewailing the meaninglessness of it all, I enjoy the brilliant absurdity of how we live. Celebrating our gonzo humanness doesn't defer the inevitable, but it brings us closer together. Our idiosyncrasies intersect like teenagers playing footsie under the table. Interrogating what it means to be a human right now is like dividing a sponge cake up with your hands – there's no clean slice to wrap in a serviette for you to take away. Everything is cantilevered by something else, like when my French teacher said, 'There's a bad apple in this class,' and looked me dead in the eye, but she was wrong because there were three of us who were too cool to behave. There's no neat wedge of internet culture, no finished mille-feuille of masculinity, no clean slate of marriage. I'm still craving a quenelle of meaning. But it's all linked and reactive like a bag of batteries with the ends occasionally touching. Civilian life is a semaphore of self-expression. Our lives are Cobb salads (like the one I'll order at The Wolseley in my pinchy shoes): disparate ingredients that make up our personal serving of modernity. Leftovers from the past thrown together with a splash of dressing somehow bringing together the components: an eaten mess. We pursue the morsels of cultural success with the fervour of a law student, ultimately rustling up a buffet of the self that we keep adding to. And we're never full. We're all American psychos now: internal monologues and extreme skincare. Laughable in 1991, but now it seems a little lacklustre. An exfoliating gel scrub and a moisturiser ... Where's the toner, Patrick?

And what's our legacy? As individuals and as communities? My mind naturally turns to offspring, because I'm at that age and parents always say their best work is their kids. I know I'll look back on these parents-in-waiting years as glorious – all the independence, all the travel, the easy logistics of two people. But without our kids we're in a twilight, an adulthood *aperitivo*: full of anticipation for the parenting ahead. Kids are a new what-if in a life of what-if. After all the coupling up and building and renovating, what if we never quite manage to have kids? Does my worldview matter if it turns to dust with me in my coffin? What's all the learning worth if I've nobody to teach?

I still have more questions than answers, some of which will never get neatly solved on the last page like an Agatha Christie where the murderer caves and spills the beans after some light questioning. I would savour the sweet catharsis of Poirot dragging the meaning of life from a room of gathered suspects. In the meantime, *aperitivo*.

Acknowledgements

Trying to remember all the people who supported this book is like naming Jesus' disciples without a Bible to hand, or all the reindeer that aren't Rudolph.

To all who know me: I appreciate the great depths of patience it takes to have me in your life and for that I thank you.